PRAISE FOR
MYSTICISM, MAGIC, AND MONASTERIES

"C.S. Lewis once said that we live in an age of 'evil enchantment,' by which he meant that we have now lived for so long within the modern paradigm that even we religious people are default materialists in how we live our lives and feel about the world, even if we 'know better' in terms of doctrine. We need a strong 'counter-spell' to wake us up from this dogmatic slumber. And Sebastian Morello has provided us with this remarkable and heartfelt book to help! I feel blessed to be living at a time in which the established paradigm is cracking up and Christianity is undergoing a rewilding. Old things are new again."

—JASON BAXTER, author of *An Introduction to Christian Mysticism: Recovering the Wildness of Spiritual Life*

"If the story of modernity has been one of 'comprehensive disenchantment' (as Charles Taylor put it), we now stand on the cusp of enchantment's return. To survive the world that will result, in which angels and demons mingle with robot dogs and silicone 'intelligences,' we will need all the metaphysical resources we can muster. Sebastian Morello's Christian counter-history of modern mysticism is an invaluable tool in the arsenal of anyone who wishes to stay sane amid a world whose longstanding 'secular' foundations are crumbling beneath us."

—MARY HARRINGTON, author of *Feminism Against Progress*

"This book opens up some of the most important but ignored questions, engaging some of the most important yet neglected resources, in the cultural and philosophical debate of our age."

—JOSEPH SHAW, author of *The Liturgy, the Family, and the Crisis of Modernity*

MYSTICISM, MAGIC, AND MONASTERIES

MYSTICISM, MAGIC, & M⊙NASTERIES

RECOVERING THE SACRED MYSTERY AT THE HEART OF REALITY

SEBASTIAN MORELLO

Foreword by Charles Coulombe

⊙'s Justi Press

Os Justi Press
P.O. Box 21814
Lincoln, NE 68542
www.osjustipress.com

Send inquiries to
info@osjustipress.com

ISBN 978-1-965303-04-7 (paperback)
ISBN 978-1-965303-05-4 (hardcover)
ISBN 978-1-965303-06-1 (ebook)

Cover and interior by Michael Schrauzer
Cover image:
Detail from Hildegard of Bingen (c. 1098–1179),
Liber Divinorum Operum, Part 1, Vision 1:
Theophany of Divine Love
Biblioteca Statale di Lucca, MS 1942

For Seraphine, Ferdinand and Roman,
in gratitude for continually revealing
to me the world's magic

CONTENTS

FOREWORD

> Those who become solitary in order to seek pro-
> fundity may reach on their path of spiritual expe-
> rience to the unshakeable insight that the dogmas
> of the Church are absolutely true.
> —Valentin Tomberg, *Lazarus, Come Forth!*

YOU hold in your hands a remarkable book, which
is destined to arouse controversy. From Descartes
on, the author tackles a number of sacred cows
dear to traditional and modernist Catholics alike. Yet
he never does so for the mere purpose of condemnation,
but to find what he conceives to be the major problem
facing the Church today and discern what solutions
there may be. He writes at a time when the various
challenges facing Church and State are rising to a fever
pitch, and all sorts of odd words, from "re-enchantment"
to "integralism," are being thrown around as possible
solutions—and receiving rancorous attacks in return.

It would be fair to say that Sebastian Morello's main
target is materialism in all its forms, some of which are
cleverly concealed—even as erroneous spirituality. But
his reading of the various situations confronting us is
never simplistic. Where some would conflate Catholicism with all other religions in an amorphous common
"tradition," he is very clear as to where Catholic truth
is; where others would see no trace of the Faith anywhere else, he shows us that those with eyes to see will
understand the foreshadowing of the Faith in other
religions, and the remnants thereof remaining therein.
At the same time, he understands that these remnants
do not render the given religion either true or salvific.

Morello's account of the Truth is wide-ranging over
space and time. He looks into the Holy Scriptures and
the Fathers, the Neoplatonists, the Romantics, and the

eighteenth- and nineteenth-century counter-revolutionary writers, while creatively engaging with contemporary scholarship. He does not scruple to look at the so-called "Perennialists" and the "Western Esoteric Tradition" in seeking answers to the questions facing us as a Church and as individuals. But Morello is quite aware that there is much chaff here; investigating the philosophies of people considered "magicians" in their day to see what truth they hold, if any, is not the same as embracing the practice of magic.

Morello would not allow me to get away with that last sentence, however, unless I defined my terms. What do I mean by magic? For that matter, what do I mean by philosophy? Here we find another of his opponents alongside materialism: sloppy thought masquerading as rectitude. For Morello, the sort of "guilt by association" that we all deplore when Christmas trees are dismissed as belonging to pagan practice is just as wrongheaded as condemning, for example, Pico della Mirandola as a Renaissance magus.

Ultimately, our author is striving to reconstruct a cohesive sense of Catholic truth, which he believes has been banished in favour of varying degrees of reductionism. For him, as for most Catholics in most times and places, the Faith is an amazing, open, and yet mysterious manner of living as well as believing, centred on the redemption of fallen man by divine grace, in a universe that is at once a reflection of its Creator, and under His sovereignty. To that end, both as individuals and as families, tribes, nations, and so on, fallen mankind has attempted to respond to the Creator's call, and to be divinised in return. Both the physical and spiritual realms must be encompassed in this quest, and neither is to be disregarded. Thus, Morello strives to avoid the twin traps of overvaluing or entirely ignoring either the spiritual or the physical realms, seeing them as correlated principles of a whole. In this view, there is no element of life that is irrelevant to the Church and her mission: from cuisine, to folklore, to civil governance, all of life is linked to the Church one way or another.

Against this all-encompassing view is the practical reduction of the redemptive reality of Christianity—especially Catholic Christianity—to a catalogue of intellectual propositions. In time, the sacraments lose their efficacy, the miraculous becomes irrelevant, and at last, as Pope Benedict XVI observed, life is reduced to a sort of pragmatic universalism by which we are saved by personal "niceness." The downside, as that Pontiff informed us, is that there is then no longer any reason to evangelise. While this sort of thinking has reached in our time a nadir of sorts in the "anonymous Christianity" of Karl Rahner and the near complete collapse of independent Catholic social politics, it has in fact been with us a long time in the form of a suspicion of the miraculous and the otherworldliness of the Faith.

In his masterful *History of the Church*, the French writer Fernand Mourret, although praising German Romanticist Joseph Görres's 1836–1842 work *Christian Mysticism*, primly cautions:

> In Görres's four volumes of *Christliche Mystik*, science abounds and scholarship overflows. But an impression of confusion comes from a reading of this encyclopaedia of all the marvels, divine and diabolical, in which ecstatics relate their visions, the stigmatists exhibit the sight of their bleeding dolours, the possessed yell in their contortions, and witches celebrate their infernal sabbaths.

This disdainful point of view was very common in the years preceding the Second Vatican Council, when even the most conservative of writers would espouse similar sentiments. Morello contends that this mindset largely led to the post-conciliar debacle. In an era when the most cutting-edge science has just confirmed the authenticity of the Shroud of Turin and confesses itself aghast at the bizarre and "impossible" qualities of several of the most recent Eucharistic miracles, such a levelled and desupernaturalised worldview is not merely an impediment to the Faith, it is flat-out wrong.

That said, Morello's approach to the Faith does not merely focus on the miraculous. Catholic social teaching is extremely important to the case he builds, as are the customs and practices of the home and community. All have their specific role to play in bringing this world of ours to Christ, ultimately transforming it and us *in* Christ. It is important also to bear in mind that this vision of the world through new eyes is not for Morello some of sort of self-delusion in order to make life today more palatable. Rather, it is just the opposite—a question of seeing reality *as it really is*, of shedding the antimetaphysical delusions of modernity with which we have all been raised, and of accepting that the truth of Christ is the most real certainty in life—more real than either death or taxes.

Occasionally, we do have such glimpses of the truth. As the writer Arthur Machen put it:

> The difficulty in recording this state is this, that it is so rare an experience that no set language to express it is in existence. A shadow of its raptures and ecstasies is found in the highest poetry; there are phrases in ancient books telling of the Celtic saints that dimly hint at it; some of the old Italian masters of painting had known it, for the light of it shines in their skies and about the battlements of their cities that are founded on magic hills. But these are but broken hints.

If that realisation ever becomes common among Catholics, it shall mark a new beginning in the history of the Church and the world. It is good for us all that Morello has grasped this truth so deeply, and that he is able to share it so eloquently.

Charles A. Coulombe
Monrovia, California
September 5, 2024
St. Lawrence Justinian

PREFACE

THOSE who know me, know that I have long harboured esoteric interests. When I taught at a catechetical institute in London, I was always accompanied to work by my whippet Pico, named after the fifteenth-century Christian Hermeticist Giovanni Pico della Mirandola, a man whom St. Thomas More described as "a perfect philosopher and a perfect theologian."[1] The name which I affectionately bestowed upon my familiar was partly to signal to the initiated that I too was a lover of the Secret Fire.

The shallowness of our age entails that in the academy at large, the Western esoteric tradition is treated with scorn and even ridicule. That, it seems, is easier than undertaking the hard work of trying to understand it. In turn, whilst I unceasingly drew on the Neoplatonic, Hermetic, and esoteric traditions in my philosophising and theologising, I tended to allude to such interests only implicitly. But after I was prevented from taking up a senior fellowship at Princeton University in 2020 on account of my critical stance towards the novel and experimental COVID-19 "vaccines," I realised that I no longer wanted to curry favour with the elite but foundering institutions of academe.

Like the Earl of Mirandola in his Florentine tower, unearthing the *prisca theologia*—the primordial theology underpinning all natural religion, illumined and transfigured by the renewing power of grace—I committed myself to seeking some understanding of our current civilisational crisis in the light of perennial wisdom (though in my case from a wooden hut in my garden, and in twenty-first century rural England). Examining the infelicitous situation in which we in the West have

---

[1] Thomas More, *The Life of Pico* (New York: Scepter Publishers, 2010), 8.

found ourselves, condemned to observe the final stages of our collapsing civilisation, I sought understanding *within* the wisdom tradition from which we've been sundered.

Some of my Catholic coreligionists deem the perennialist traditionalism for which I have much sympathy to be suspect. But I think this is generally for one of two reasons. Either they associate it with the more unconventional interests of the Renaissance Christian humanists, which included Jewish Kabbalah and practical alchemy; or they see it to be bound up with the Freemasonry that largely inspired the revolutionism of the eighteenth and nineteenth centuries. In any case, they consider *all* occult knowledge to belong to the dark occult.

The traditionalism to which I refer, however, is based on little more than the acknowledgement that in man's nature there is a wisdom, woven into the very constitution of our species, there from when God wandered with Adam in the Garden. And whilst sin has obscured this wisdom, it is nonetheless still present, to be treated with seriousness and respect. For this reason, the Christian humanists of the Quattrocento—especially Pico and Marsilio Ficino—sought with great energy to reconcile the natural wisdom they were uncovering in the Platonic, Neoplatonic, and Hermetic traditions with the supernatural revelation of which they deemed the Church the true guardian. And later, counter-revolutionaries like Edmund Burke, Louis de Bonald, and Joseph de Maistre, in the face of modernity's evils, utilised the insights of perennialist traditionalism in defence of Christianity and the civilisation it had sacralised and vivified. One way to put this is that this school of thought from which I draw simply expands the notion of *synderesis*—the unexamined intellectual habits of practical wisdom—from individual persons to corporate persons, tracing the intuitively held truths of the shared minds of civilisations. Indeed, this is precisely what John Henry Newman describes in a letter of 1829:

> As each individual has certain instincts of right
> and wrong antecedently to reasoning, on which
> he acts—and rightly so—which perverse reasoning
> may supplant, which then can hardly be regained,
> but if regained will be regained from a different
> source—from reasoning, not from nature—so, I
> think, has the world of men collectively. God gave
> them truths in His miraculous revelations, and
> other truths in the unsophisticated infancy of
> nations, scarcely less necessary and divine. These
> are transmitted as 'the wisdom of our ancestors'
> through men, many of whom cannot enter into
> them, or receive them themselves—still on, on,
> from age to age, not the less truths because many
> of the generations through which they are trans-
> mitted are unable to prove them, but hold them,
> either from pious and honest feeling (it may be)
> or from bigotry or from prejudice. That they are
> truths it is most difficult to prove, for great men
> alone can prove great ideas or grasp them....
> Moral truth is gained by patient study, by calm
> reflection, silently as the dew falls—unless mirac-
> ulously given—and when gained it is transmitted
> by faith and by 'prejudice.'[2]

There is a shared wisdom, claims Newman, which is
imparted to man's nature by his Author, which is tacitly
known only in the collective mind of corporate persons
such as nations and civilisations down the ages. This
"wisdom of our ancestors," to use Newman's words, is
not rationally articulated and demonstrably proven, but
received implicitly, through culture, custom, and habit.
Indeed, Newman says that this wisdom is possessed by
prejudice, a word which, just as it didn't for Edmund
Burke, connotes in principle nothing shameful for Newman—as it does not for me. (It is this ancestral wisdom,
and how it is passed on and received, that I explore in
my own way in the chapter entitled "On Killing Our
Elders" in this volume.)

---

[2] John Henry Newman, *Letters and Correspondence*, I, 179–180, www.
newmanreader.org/biography/mozley/volume1/file5.html.

Natural wisdom finds its summit in natural religion—that is, in the religious impulse in the depths of man which supernatural religion comes by revelation and grace to illumine and transform. Hence, if we get nature wrong, we will get supernature skewed. And for this reason, as Christopher Dawson convincingly argued, Newman thought that rehabilitating true natural religion was a fundamental prerequisite for combatting the phoney "natural religion" of the Enlightenment *philosophes* and the revolutionist epoch which they birthed.[3] Thus, Dawson does not hesitate to associate Newman with Maistre, Bonald, and other eighteenth- and nineteenth-century counter-revolutionaries whose "traditionalism" he says Newman's own "strikingly resembles."[4] And it is that traditionalism of the French Catholic counter-revolutionaries that some scholars have placed at the genesis of the whole perennialist, esoteric revival that endures into our own time, and which continues to be concerned with the visible—exoteric, if you like—crisis of our civilisational collapse.[5] Unfortunately, due to the foolish but widespread conflation of moral progress with technological innovation, many do not realise that any such collapse is underway, when in fact we are in its final convulsions.

In the struggle to survive our civilisation's rapid unravelling, we will have to contend with the rise of *goetia*—that is, of sorcery—among those intent on enslaving us. Certainly, from its inception, modernity has been satanical, but, as C. S. Lewis famously noted in his *Screwtape Letters*, not always overtly so. More recently, however, our epoch has become openly and visibly demonic in its music, fashions, moral commitments, bodily mutilations, and paraliturgies. My personal response, perhaps more

---

[3] Christopher Dawson, *The Spirit of the Oxford Movement* (Washington, DC: The Catholic University of America Press, 2023), 30.
[4] Dawson, 30.
[5] See Thomas Garrett Isham, *Contra Mundum: Joseph de Maistre and the Birth of Tradition* (Kettering, OH: Angelico Press/Sophia Perennis, 2017).

through disgust at what I observe than by any chosen decision on my part, has been to double-down on my obstinate traditionalism in all things: in religion, in aesthetics, in culture, in morals, and in everything else.

As an unapologetic traditionalist, I found a home at *The European Conservative*, a journal for which I became a senior editor, an editorial board member, and a regular writer and filmmaker. And it was at this journal that I was given the freedom to explore my esoteric, Hermetic, Neoplatonic penchants, free from the unwholesome prejudices of the modern university. It remains my conviction that esoteric transformation and exoteric transformation are correlative transformations, and in turn that there exists a deep and inescapable relationship between the spiritual and the political. Modernity's attempt to sever these two has largely failed and will fail ultimately, as will all of modernity's various attempts to undercut reality. But when the whole illusory edifice of our progressivist regime topples, wise people will be needed amid the ensuing challenges. Such people, it seems to me, will be those who spent the time of their civilisation's disintegration inducting themselves deep, deep, deep into the eternal wisdom disclosed in the created order, and in a knowledge of the marvellous encounter of that order with the divine grace that comes from without to renew it.

Who knows if we are witnessing the diabolical principality's final onslaught against the remnants of what we once called Christendom? What we *do* know is that the Church has always taught that the world is an arena of strife, wherein the devil's principality and the Lord's Kingdom are in ongoing conflict. The baptised, it seems to me, are unfit to defend their Kingdom whilst they remain under so many spells, the spells of modernity. Breaking those spells, or at least exposing them, is largely the purpose of this book.

A word about the cover. My case in this book, among

other things, is that traditionalists receive a hard time in the institutional Church partly because her acceptance of modernity has meant that she has grown alien to herself. In turn, a cover image was needed that would be both strange to modern-day Catholic sensibilities and yet very much of the Church's Tradition. For me, this meant one of the shimmering and symbolically-rich images found in St. Hildegard von Bingen's manuscripts, each representing one of her many mystical visions. Of all these images, that of the red angel, called "The Theophany of Divine Love," is perhaps my favourite. Following the method of Abbot Trithemius—though not quite with the rigorous asceticism that he recommends—of late I have been meditating on this image to draw closer to the loving spirits who accompany us. The image is a catechesis: the angelic mind is given a share in the divine mind of God, and with divine knowledge received in the manifold graces of the heavenly mansions, the angel descends in the royal robes of the celestial court. All crimson with the fire of God's love, the potent spirit enters our earthly order with the Word of God as a double-edged sword, and he mediates the graces derived from the Lamb's sacrifice, for the transformation of the world. By this revelation and grace, whose symbols he holds to his heart, he guards the baptised, crushing the demons who assail them and delivering them from their sinful inclinations, symbolised by the twining serpent. The image, then, is a whole theology on angelic operation and presence, without which we would surely be lost, unable to find our way at all.

ACKNOWLEDGEMENTS

M Y thanks to my wife and children, who are my world. My profoundest gratitude to Mario and Ellen Fantini, in whose journal, *The European Conservative*, first appeared many of the essays that were eventually adapted into the chapters of this book. Peter Kwasniewski proposed that this volume be produced, and I am thankful to him and to his press, Os Justi, for making it all happen; Peter is not only a friend but perhaps the foremost living defender of our Holy Tradition, and anyone who cares about the integrity of the Church's liturgical life—which is life itself—owes him a tremendous debt of gratitude. My deepest thanks to Charles Coulombe for his wonderful Foreword, which provides a helpful initiatory pathway into this book's spirit. I thank many others who have been of especial importance to me in the formation of the ideas found in this book, and who, by virtue of their sympathy with an approach to the philosophy of religion that privileges the contributions of mysticism, sophiology, Neoplatonism, and Hermeticism, did not merely raise their eyebrows. In this regard, I especially thank Michael Martin, Brian Scarffe, Joseph Shaw, Francis and Annabel Osborn, Daniel Samuel, John Vervaeke, Mary Harrington, Fr Charbel Hars, Alicja Gescinska, Roger Buck, John Rao, Pierpaolo Finaldi, Theo Howard, and of course my fellow adventurers Peter Jones and Clive Watson.

INTRODUCTION

THE reader will have to forgive the self-referential character of this book's beginnings, but on account of its unusual contents, at least in parts, a personal apologia seems necessary. You see, my initial formal training was in strict scholasticism. The object of philosophical enquiry was deemed to be truth, and truth was whatever Garrigou-Lagrange judged it to be. With such training came the advantage of a certain rigour, and the disadvantage of a somewhat encaged mind. This intellectual confinement was not without its emotional challenges; years earlier, having escaped an English boarding school where I'd been held for three years, I enrolled at an arts college to train for the stage, which opened to me a whole narrative-based mode of humane learning which I found both transformative and liberating. But repelled by the combined competitiveness and superficiality of the theatrical trade, I slowly grew to be tormented by the "big questions," and consequently started reading works of philosophy and comparative religion, topics on which my father had accumulated an extensive library over the years, of which I took full advantage. This mounting interest eventually took me East. I wandered the Himalayas and the Indian subcontinent, sleeping in temples, immersing myself in practical Hinduism and yoga, and studying Tibetan Buddhism at Dharamshala, regularly attending addresses by the Dalai Lama and other senior monks of that tradition. I witnessed man's universal search for wisdom, particularised in the great traditions of the world. Thus, when I finally came to undertake philosophy degrees later in life, I quickly intuited the danger of stuffing the magic and mystery of the cosmos into a tidy set of abstract formulae, that danger being spiritual blindness.

Later in my studies, seeking cognitive unshackling from the partialities of rationalism, I threw myself into the works of the sixteenth-century Salamancan scholars and their fascinating debates over the liberties of the Amerindians before an encroaching Spanish empire. Soon after that, I became enthralled by the Italian and northern Renaissance humanists, and to my astonishment I discovered that far from a break with St. Thomas Aquinas and the medieval schoolmen, figures such as Thomas More and John Fisher in England and Pico della Mirandola and Marsilio Ficino in the Italian peninsula deemed themselves followers of the Angelic Doctor. Thomas More called Aquinas "the flower of theology,"[1] Fisher created a complex system at Cambridge of integrating the "new learning" into the ontology of Aquinas,[2] Pico devoted 45 of his *Nine-hundred Theses* to defending Aquinas's metaphysics,[3] and Ficino—as I discuss later in this volume—was the foremost Renaissance thinker to uncover the Neoplatonic structure of emanation and participation undergirding Aquinas's wider theology.

By the time I came to write *The World as God's Icon: Creator and Creation in the Platonic Thought of Thomas Aquinas*, eventually published by Angelico Press in 2020, it was clear to me that there was a lot more to Aquinas than what his modern commentators had to say about him. Indeed, perhaps no other premodern author has so suffered the indignity of posthumously having modernity read into his works. In the Common Doctor, free as he now was from the mechanistic and rationalistic assumptions that I had previously learned to impose upon him, I found the armoury I needed for the intellectual assault

---

[1] Thomas More, "Confutation of Tyndale's Answer," in *The Complete Works of St. Thomas More* (New Haven, CT: Yale University Press, 1997), VIII:713.
[2] See Richard Rex, *The Theology of John Fisher* (Cambridge: Cambridge University Press, 2003), 1.
[3] See Paul Oskar Kristella, *Medieval Aspects of Renaissance Learning* (Durham, NC: Duke University Press, 1974), 72.

on modernity that I had longed to launch. Modernity, it was clear to me, was one long attack on wisdom, and it was to wisdom that I wished to give my life. This, then, led me to undertake my doctoral research on "religion by establishment," which was really an extended case against all revolutionary politics and ethics, subsequently published in 2023 as a Routledge monograph entitled *Conservatism and Grace*. While researching for this work, I determined that modernity is an attack not only on wisdom *per se*, but on wisdom embodied in persons. Indeed, modernity is, I would come to argue, the very name for the process of depersonalisation discernible all around us in our epoch. And incidentally, for this research project, I also had to undergo initiation into the Hermetic mind of Joseph de Maistre, an intellectual adventure which did not leave me unchanged.

Modernity, I have come to see, is ultimately a conjuring of black magic by which the mind is hexed with abstractionism, rationalism, scientism, mechanisation, and all the various ways we are rendered sightless by the blinding of the mind's eye. The universe, in turn, has ceased to be a meeting place of God and man, and has become lifeless *stuff* to be utilised—for what ultimate end we do not know, and nor do we trouble ourselves with such a question. We have, consequently, become a people without wisdom, and given that wisdom is the lifeblood of the mind and the animator of the heart, we are rightly judged dead. As many have pointed out in recent years, that is likely why the only mythos that late modernity has been able to produce (and reproduce in a thousand different ways) is that of the "zombie apocalypse," for such a mythos cathartically and allegorically presents to us our current condition.

The antithesis of seeing the world with the eyes of a zombie—that is, with the eyes of a soulless consumer who mindlessly devours all life he encounters—is that of apprehending the world as *living*, as God's own theophanic self-communication, and as the primordial cosmic liturgy. This "sophianic vision"—though I did not put it like that at the time—is what I discovered Aquinas's ontology to entail, what the Christian humanists of the Northern Renaissance knew the Protestant revolt would eclipse, and what the counter-revolutionaries of the eighteenth century understood the rise of ideology in modernity would finally eradicate—sweeping away Christendom with it.

Part of adopting a premodern mind is first acknowledging that every people in history has accepted that our world is a world pregnant with magical forces and the activity of spiritual beings. And Christianity has never denied that curses, hexes, and many kinds of evil spells exist, or that evil spirits can be contacted and succumbed to, in order to attain evil ends. So too, Christians—alongside their practices of meditation and contemplation—have ever believed in sacred magic, or "theurgy," but they have held that such magic possesses the power to conquer demons and sacralise the world only when united to the eternal and singular priesthood of Jesus Christ, and to this baptised theurgy Christians have given the name of *liturgy*. This brings us to the great political work to which Christians ought to be dedicated, namely the endeavour to establish liturgical nations in fraternal union with each other, for the alternative to such a civilisation is the accursed dominion in which nations are first fragmented and then dissolved altogether in the grey mass of a diabolical slave settlement.

I naturally looked for the sophianic vision of creation as theophany among other writers. And I found that this "submerged reality," as my friend Michael Martin calls it, has been consistently defended in recent decades by fellow Catholic authors who have been especially sensitive to the evils of rationalism and its corrosive effects.[4]

---

[4] See Michael Martin, *The Submerged Reality: Sophiology and the Turn to a Poetic Metaphysics* (Brooklyn, NY: Angelico Press, 2015).

Accordingly, I came to immerse myself in the writings of thinkers such as Valentin Tomberg, Jean Hani, Jean Borella, and Wolfgang Smith. The importance of these authors and others who have uncovered the mystical foundations of reality cannot be overstated. Moreover, their intellectual project has not been merely a speculative one, but one which takes seriously the practical consequences of their endeavours. For if the created order is the self-communication of God, then, if I may put it this way, we might be called to *reply*. Hence, what these authors and others like them reveal is the path not only to an encounter with ultimate reality through the various levels of reality, but to opening one's heart to grace by initiation into that which grace comes to transform—namely all *nature*—and thus to personal transformation in loving communion with reality's Source: God Himself. As it was for the theurgical masters and philosophers of the ancient Mediterranean, so the path of Sophia becomes for us one of mystical union, but now baptised and rendered intimate in the mystery of the Incarnation.

It is for the reason just sketched that at times in this volume I am especially preoccupied with the distinction between the natural and the supernatural. Christianity is haunted by failures with regard to this distinction. The Eastern Orthodox have long rejected the mediating category of "created supernature" (grace), opting rather for the somewhat ambiguous essence-*energeia* division of Gregory Palamas, the unhappy practical corollaries of which this isn't the place to examine. Protestantism got rid of nature as a species of revelation altogether and thereby opened the pathway to seeing creation as mere *stuff*, accelerating the onset of modernity's dead, mechanistic universe. By so doing, not only did Protestantism lose any vision of nature, but it lost a biblical account of grace as well. Catholic Christianity hasn't fared much better. At times Catholicism has so radically separated nature and grace that the Christian is viewed as a two-lives spiritual schizophrenic, with the world around him reduced to mere *stuff*, rendering Catholics little wiser than the most closed-minded Protestants. At other times Catholicism has so conflated nature and grace that it has collapsed one into the other, with creation understood as supernatural in and of itself, or grace understood as natural, which amount to the same thing. I am convinced that our account of grace—which after all is only the theological term for what St. Peter calls becoming "partakers in the divine nature" (1 Peter 1:4)—will remain a mess, and Catholics will continue to oscillate between these two errors, until we first get our account of nature right, and thus get right what grace enters history from without to transform. And nature isn't *stuff* at all, it turns out, but divine music. Yes, divine music thrown out of tune by rebellion and disobedience, but also brought back into beautiful harmony with the intervention of Him whose music it is, and by His glorious love we are all given a part to sing.

It should be obvious from the view of creation that I have just conveyed that I am deeply suspicious of any kind of "mysticism" that is understood as a spiritual "ascent" out of the created order and towards a Deity grasped as unconnected from the world around us. The kind of Aristotelianism that treats the realm of the senses as the only apposite reality, and the kind of Platonism that treats the realm of the senses as illusory, appear to me equally problematic. Neoplatonism was a tremendous corrective to these misapprehensions. Through seeing the world as intelligible insofar as it participates in the mind of God, and existent insofar as it emanates from the mind of God and is willed into being at all times by Him, Neoplatonism—which had its origins in a philosophical school that competed with the Church for supremacy in the Greco-Roman

world—provided to the Church the metaphysical structure it required to comprehend the view of creation it
had received in narrative form through the Holy Scriptures. That, indeed, is one of the great ironies of the
history of our civilisation.

The mystico-philosophy of Neoplatonism and the
revelation of the Christian religion were synthesised in
the early Church and together became the foundations
of theology, both Latin and Greek, in the Patristic age. To
the degree that we have departed from those foundations,
our theology has become degraded by admixture with
ideology—a sacrilegious tragedy fully observable in the
theology departments of today's universities. Authentic
mysticism is not a gnostic departure from the created
order of which we are in any case an inextricable part.
Rather, mysticism depends on understanding created
reality as the dynamic declaration of God, of which
we are all addressees, and consequently uniting ourselves—or better, allowing ourselves to be united—to
the One who speaks.

I have often thought that the seventeenth-century
Dutch artist Johannes Vermeer must have been something of a mystical master. It was once thought by art
historians that he converted to Catholicism only due to
marrying into a Catholic family, but more recently others
have claimed that he must have made the choice on
account of personal religious conviction. Vermeer's ten
surviving children were all named after saints to whom
the family had personal devotions; he moved his family
next-door to a hidden Jesuit church in Amsterdam, where
they could regularly attend clandestine liturgies; and
increasingly there is speculation about the significance
of his only explicitly religious painting. The painting
in question, entitled *The Allegory of Faith* (Plate 1), was
painted soon after Vermeer's conversion to Catholicism.
The image is that of a woman in mystical ecstasy, with
a chalice, a crucifix, and the Holy Scriptures open on

PLATE 1
Johannes Vermeer, *The Allegory of Faith* (c. 1670)
Metropolitan Museum of Art, New York

a table before her, and a globe under her foot. A large image of Calvary hangs on the wall behind the woman, and in the foreground lies a crushed serpent, whose blood runs towards the viewer.

Numerous enthusiasts claim that *The Allegory of Faith* is of especial importance as Vermeer's one religious painting, and certainly much can be learned about his view of spiritual transformation therefrom: the serpent has been conquered; the woman's hand is suspended over her pounding heart as she is drawn into the love of God through meditating on the Scriptures and steeping herself in the sacramental life—symbolised by the objects on the table—by which her whole existence is grasped in the light of Christ's redeeming power. Indeed, she seems almost draped in the image of Calvary behind her. There is much here on which to meditate, but in fact I wish to suggest that *all* of Vermeer's paintings are equally religious, albeit in a different way. For what the art of Vermeer reveals is that even the most mundane, quotidian, in-the-world activities—like pouring some milk or tasting a new wine—are in fact infused with divine meaning and purpose, for those who have eyes to see. Vermeer is truly the artist of the "sacrament of the present moment," and that is surely why in *The Allegory of Faith*, as the woman (a representation of the Christian soul) is whirled up into union with the infinite love of God, she remains anchored by her foot in *this* world where she encounters that love.

Many of my readers follow my writing especially for my meditations on hunting and other outdoor pursuits. But my love of hunting—and my general attachment to the landscape—is not disconnected from my understanding of the interior life. Rather, it gets to the heart of it. For inasmuch as I condemn the modern sundering of the spiritual and political, so too I equally condemn the severing of the spiritual and the ecological. Put plainly, a true mystic is necessarily also a conservationist.

As it is for Vermeer's raptured soul, personified in *The Allegory of Faith*, so I see mystical experience as arising from having one's foot firmly on the earth. And thus, like Roger Scruton and his "totemic foxes," I see ethical hunting in particular as a profoundly spiritual activity.[5] It is through hunting that I speak the language of the animals, I enter into nature's cycle, and I move amongst the prowling predators of the world—but as a human, unique among predators, I can enjoy a moral relation with my prey, seeking both to minimise its suffering and to honour it in its sacrifice. As Michael Martin, to whom I referred above, puts it in a glorious poem that he wrote whilst sitting in his hide, rifle in hand, waiting for a white tail buck:

> I've opened apple trees to air and light
> With a pruning knife, revealing cathedrals
> Hidden in their branches: there I first learned
> Contemplation and received a transfigured face.[6]

It is this conception of the world as a realm that, when known properly, reveals itself to be a cathedral, that I repeatedly attempt to defend throughout this book. Again, creation is the emanation of the Godhead—a true source of revelation—and as such, at the most fundamental level, the cosmos is inherently and intrinsically *personal*. To realise that the cosmos is God's iconography is to be in right relation with it, which is the first step on the path to right relationality with its Source, Who, like Francis Thompson's *Hound of Heaven*, is ever pursuing us through its arboreal ways.[7] Then, one enters

---

[5] See Roger Scruton, *On Hunting* (London: Yellow Jersey Press, 1999), 68–79.
[6] Michael Martin, "Trees. Water. Fire." in *Mythologies of the Wild of God* (Brooklyn, NY: Angelico Press, 2024), 10–11.
[7] In a similar vein, the philosopher Jean Hani, in an analysis of the various symbolic depictions of God as hunter that have emerged throughout Christian tradition and beyond, writes the following: "The symbol here expresses the very condition of man and of every creature in the world, a condition in which it is impossible for them in any way to escape God. To become aware of this situation and perhaps

the joy of contemplation wherein is encountered the "transfigured face." And this life of the *embodied* soul is, I suppose, the primary object of deliberation throughout this volume.

The pre-eminence of the mystical life understood not as spiritual ascent out of the created order, but rather as embodied induction into shared life with a personal God who meets us in the world that is an emanation of His own inner life, is emphasised by me largely because I observe that in the epoch of ideology—namely, modernity—we have lost a sense of the existentiality and immanence of the Sacred Mystery. Tragically, this spiritual blindness has encroached on many aspects of religious devotion and piety. In turn, religion is understood ever less as ongoing transformation through the liturgical and sacramental life, and it is instead understood as mere intellectual assent to doctrinal propositions and spiritual ascent away from the concrete reality in which we find ourselves. Religion is hence tacitly reframed for a people formed by virtual reality lived from an online existence. Unfortunately, such a life is no life at all. And the upshot is the reduction of Christianity, or whatever we mean by Christianity today, to a base species of ideology, just one among a plethora of squabbling ideologies in the modernist arena of competing "systems." The repackaging of what *should* denote the transformation of our nature by the supernatural love of the Incarnate Logos as another rationalistic modernism strikes me as nothing other than blasphemous.

I wish, then, to call my readership back to the mysticism of the concrete, to God's presence among the

---

to accept it can be, moreover, the starting point of the spiritual path, which explains how such a path may sometimes be compared to a hunt in which the soul is, as it were, 'being tracked' by God, or, inversely, is 'ardently hunting its prey, Christ' (Eckhart)." *Divine Craftsmanship: Preliminaries to a Spirituality of Work* (Kettering, OH: Angelico Press/ Sophia Perennis, 2016), 74.

pots and pans, as St. Teresa of Avila put it. The Lord walks among us. To see Him, we have only to break the spell that blinds the eyes of the spirit. When, like Tobit, through our communion with angels, the excrement of our epoch falls from our eyes, and we behold creation as it is, as a wondrous cathedral wherein the great cosmic liturgy of God's emanated goodness unfolds, we can do nothing other than praise Him. The Christian life, understood as absorption into the cosmic liturgy of the created order, reflected and redeemed by the bridal liturgy of the Church, through which the whole world calls out to its Maker in nuptial love, is the way it was lived in the Church's monastic genius. The ebbing of the role of monasticism over the centuries is in large part to blame for the lamentable condition in which the Church finds itself today. For this reason, in this volume, I bring to the fore the need for a monastic renewal in the life of the Church, which I see to be perhaps the principal practical requirement for any salvaging of our civilisation.

I invite the reader, then, to join me in re-enchanting the world; not by projecting some romantic and vague notion of spirituality onto the world by an act of sheer will, but by genuine liberation from the black magic of modernity. Then, by seeing creation as it really is, and accordingly entering the love of the Creator, we might perceive that our civilisational collapse has before all else its cause in a spiritual crisis.

1

THE LOSS OF SACRED PLACES

A WHILE ago, a short video was circulated on Catholic social media of an American priest—apparently an exorcist—answering questions from a pulpit, presumably after delivering a parish talk. In the video, a lady from the congregation asks him about the use of healing stones and crystals, saying that she has a collection of such stones and that she finds it relaxing to have them around. The priest then replies to her:

> You mean New Age energy crystals?... You should not have those. That is incompatible with the Christian faith. Inanimate objects, like crystals, don't give energy. That's a superstition. If you're feeling energy from them, then that is a sign that something is spiritually wrong.

Even on reductionist, purely physics-based grounds, the priest's answer is incorrect, as stones and crystals *do* possess energies that are measurable with scientific instruments. But that's not the point, for it is clear that the priest is objecting to the possibility that this lady might attribute to these stones a kind of spiritual power that may go beyond some mere, perceived healing effect (like the medicinal effect of copper for arthritis, for example).

It is fortunate that this priest was not a contemporary of Albert the Great or Hildegard von Bingen—both saints and doctors of the Church—as he likely would have accused them of promulgating occultism or superstition, given their interest in, and use of, so-called "energy crystals," in praise of which they both wrote a surprising amount.[1] (I recommend to the reader Hildegard's

---

[1] For a well-researched study of St. Albert the Great as a student and practitioner of sacred magic and related disciplines, see David J.

introduction to Book Four of her work *Physica*, in which you will find the following breathtaking sentence: "The devil detests...precious stones; for he remembers that their beauty was manifest on his own spiritual body before he fell from the glory that God had given him.")

Be that as it may, it seems to me that the reaction of this priest, who is clearly a member of the Catholic traditionalist movement, stems from a subterranean anthropological commitment, namely "Cartesian dualism." Despite the treacherousness of this term, it is nonetheless helpful as by it I mean what it evokes in the broadest possible sense, namely that all reality may be split into two categories, the terms of art for which are the *res extensa* and the *res cogitans*. That is to say, the world is composed of two kinds of existence, the interior realm of meaning and purpose, bound up with "the self," and the exterior realm of atomic formations, best understood by recourse to mechanistic metaphors. And it is supposed that *if* we are to possess clarity about the world, these two realms must never be confused or conflated. Indeed, in the Cartesian view, it is precisely the Neoplatonic, poetic, symbolic metaphysics of the ancients and the Church Fathers that kept us in the age of superstition— to use that priest's preferred term—for so very long.

What that priest in that widely shared video thought was that the lady was running the risk of conflating these two realms. And this is very serious, for ever since the division of the world into interior meaning and external stuff, conceived mechanistically, it is widely supposed that we have moved into a new epoch of scientific—and consequently, civilisational—progress. So, we are counselled to be careful, for the other way lies superstition, just as the priest observed. On this model, sacrality cannot be found in the realm of things, but only in the interior realm of the cloistered self where true religion lies. It seems to have gone unnoticed both by that priest and by his many online admirers that such a view gravely undermines the theory of *natural* sacramentality of which Thomas Aquinas wrote a great deal in his two *Summas*, a sacramentality which importantly prefigures the institution of supernatural sacraments and the existence of sacramentals—but more on that later.

As I suggest, the priest on whom I mercilessly pick is under the Cartesian spell. This shouldn't shock us, for it is obvious that this spell is one that has hexed the whole Church. It is unfortunate that the priest's status as an exorcist persuades the faithful that he holds an oracular position among them, thereby perpetuating the spell. But again, that should not surprise us, for once we lose—on account of Cartesian dualism—a sense of God's declaration of Himself in the created world to which we are *all* privy as its rational part, the need for gurus with elite knowledge becomes paramount. Indeed, that is why the primacy of the didactic—rather than liturgical—role of the pastor follows so seamlessly from the view found in Protestantism that the world is so utterly corrupted by the Fall that it cannot itself be a species of revelation, and why since the Catholic Church adopted Cartesianism as its dominant worldview, Catholics have by necessity taken on the likeness of Protestants. (Though, in the spirit of fairness, it ought to be acknowledged that some Lutheran thinkers, from Jacob Boehme to Ludwig Gotthard Kosegarten—the latter being the pastor whose theology inspired the romantic artist Caspar David Friedrich—sought with varied success to undo Luther's view of creation without undoing Lutheranism, but I do not count their work to have been a success in the long run.)

In any case, it is easy to trace how this need for gurus occurred. In classical metaphysics, the cosmos is comprised of substances which are themselves sharers in universality by all sharing in *being*. And the cosmos's substances—with which we're surrounded—in their particularity disclose the realm of created intelligible being in innumerable ways. The fact that substances, by existing as the things they are, disclose themselves, reveals that they necessarily find their fulfilment in mind. Given that things are inherently intelligible in this way, and thus convey their intelligibility, according to the ancients they must be emanations of mind, *Divine* Mind, and by virtue of that intelligibility they disclose themselves to our created minds. Hence, at least in the premodern worldview, the cosmos *is* divine communication, and like any communication, it is an interpersonal declaration that achieves its finality in the realm of intellect, by which in turn the realm of intellect is brought to perfection. The upshot of such a view is that anything that consequently unfolds out of *our* minds is reflective of our interconnection with being itself, and therefore with the Divine Mind in which all created beings participate. As the philosopher Joseph Milne puts it:

> The arts and the institutions of civilisation in their essential nature...embody man's apprehension of the universe and his bearing towards all that is. The arts bear witness to beauty, politics and jurisprudence to justice, cultivation of the earth and medicine to the good, and learning to truth. The degree to which these each attain their ends depends upon the depth of intellectual receptivity to all that is which prevails at any time.[2]

Of course, if what Milne says is true, then conversely, if the arts fail to bear witness to beauty, politics to justice, medical practice to human health, cultivation to conservation, or education to truth—that is to say, if a given civilisation were to become characterised by ugliness, injustice, medical malpractice, the pollution of the earth, and the dissemination of error—then this should

---

[2] Joseph Milne, *Metaphysics and the Cosmic Order* (London: The Temenos Academy, 2008), 32.

be understood as symptomatic of epistemic alienation from being itself, indeed as the divorce of mind itself from reality. (Lucky, then, that there's no indication of *that* happening around us!)

Modern man, then, lives in a darkened prison of his own making, simultaneously believing himself to see everything. Once mind and being are thus severed, as they were at the beginning of modernity—first by severing creation from the Divine Mind, making creation not an emanation of the Divine Mind but a mere artifact of Divine will—a view that fast led to deism; and second, by the Cartesian severing of the human mind from material being—it becomes difficult to see how the corporeally encaged self is supposed to navigate its way through this world, with which it has no essential connection whatever. In turn, reliance on cognoscenti who possess elite knowledge becomes paramount, and the common mind of the community is dismissed in favour of a privileged gnostic mind of an elite.

All this has of course played out in the temporal world, but it also has done so in ecclesiastical institutions. A full account of the genealogy of the Church's bewitchment by Descartes' spell is certainly beyond the scope of this chapter, even if I could achieve such a feat. But I *do* want to convince you that such a bewitchment has indeed taken place, that traditionalists no less than modernists fall prey to it, and that this bewitchment is supported by highly authoritative sources.

In the first meditation of St. Ignatius of Loyola's *Spiritual Exercises*, he asks the retreatant to imagine himself ensnared in the fleshly cage of the body, awaiting liberation. In his own words: "When a...meditation is about something abstract...the composition will be...to consider my soul as *imprisoned* in this corruptible body." Thereafter, Ignatius repeatedly asks the retreatant to reflect upon himself, analyse himself, enter into himself. A recurrent motif of the whole work of the *Exercises* is this notion of the cloistered "self" occupied with interior interaction with the cloistered "self."

Ignatius's order is widely credited with leading the charge against the Protestant revolution, and no doubt it did. But fascinatingly, the anthropology of the so-called reformers, namely that of the "inner self" making a personal religious commitment—rather than the integral, relational *person* being sanctified by induction into a visible and liturgical community—is reflected precisely in the anthropology and consequent spirituality of Ignatius and his followers.[3]

As I shall argue at greater length in chapter 9, many of the Church's modern maladies are due to the institution's transition over the centuries from a monastic culture to a clerical culture. This entailed a slow change from a culture of stable, liturgical communities to a culture of frequently moving preachers with lives distanced from those of the lay faithful. Indeed, arguably it was the Jesuits who above all changed mainstream western Christianity from a liturgical religion to a religion of personal piety: one of spiritual exercises, novenas, chaplets, mortifications, visits to the Blessed Sacrament, and a certain fixation on private revelations, all markedly detached from the liturgical year. Certainly, these things are not bad in themselves, but with the rise of this spirituality was seen a change in Latin soteriology, a shift from the sanctification of a spiritual nation—namely the new Israel, the Church—to the "sanctification of souls," as it is said. This process has seemingly reached a climax in our own age with the widespread reduction of Catholic practice to a kind of ongoing therapeutic self-affirmation exercise.

Thus, the Church's culture moved from one focused on the supernatural transformation of concrete localities and communities to the sanctification of the interior life

---

[3] The fact that the Jesuits were dispensed, for the first time in church history, from the choral recitation of the Divine Office is symptomatic of the shift. The Office shifted from a chanted public liturgy to a recited breviary for the individual to read on his own.

and the inner self, shifting the emphasis from shared places and communal practices to personal piety and rational assent to propositions. To be clear, I do not place *all* the responsibility in this process on Ignatius and his Jesuits, or any one person or group. With regard to the Church's Cartesian bewitchment and its precursors, the shift from privileging object to subject was increasingly in the very drinking water, so to speak. I am merely noting that this shift, from incarnational and communal religiosity to that of the inner self was one tacitly adopted by the Church's most influential order in the modern age, and that this is relevant for understanding how we arrived at where we are.

However much you may agree or disagree with me regarding this process of subjectification and who or what may have been responsible for it, you can well imagine the young René Descartes during his early education among the Jesuits, when he had to undertake regular retreats according to an abbreviated form of Ignatius's *Exercises*, being impressed by Ignatius's image of the ghostly self in the fleshly prison. But certainly, what became Cartesian anthropology and its accompanying epistemology, to name it, *rationalism*, had for some time been growing in the culture of the West. I emphasise this because I see *events* and *relationships* as possessing much more causal power, and hence explanatory power for discernible historical changes, than mere ideas.

As it happens, I consider the modern proclivity for attributing inordinate causal power to ideas to be an effect of seeing the *res cogitans* as the true reality to be privileged above the "stuff" with which we're surrounded. If there is one thing that studying and teaching philosophy for nearly two decades has taught me, it is that ideas really aren't that important. When philosophers attribute much causal power to their ideas, as Descartes repeatedly did in droves—claiming that all subsequent history and thought would be different purely on account of his

arguments—I deem that conceit, and Descartes' character
certainly contained a generous helping of conceit. (Fortunately, I have been delivered from such conceit by long
observing that my own ideas produce no effects at all.)

I cannot emphasise this enough: I really do think
that philosophy's content is principally *post hoc* and
retrospective, and not efficient and instrumental, and
I see philosophical content in each age to be normally
explicable by reference to prior historical events or
sequences. So, in the case of Descartes, rather than
launching a new method, as he thought he was doing,
I think he was in fact offering an abstract account
of what had already largely happened to the Western
mind—as I have said, already detectible in Ignatius's
spirituality. It had happened, I think, chiefly due to
two great causes of uprootedness—for uprootedness
always leads to inordinate abstractionism—those two
causes being the warfare and population movement that
characterised the sixteenth and seventeenth centuries.

If the assumptions that were articulated by Descartes
had been growing dominant for quite some time before
he wrote them up as an overt worldview—as the Western
mind had incrementally become the modern mind—by
mid-modernity our civilisation was saturated in them.
Let me give you an example of the kind of thing I
mean.[4] The language scholar Logan Pearsall Smith notes
in his book *The English Language* that a group of words
appeared for the first time in the eighteenth century,
which he describes in the following way: "A curious class
of verbs and adjectives which describe not so much the
objective qualities and activities of things, as the effects
they produce in us." In the list he offers, he includes
the adjectives "entertaining," "exhilarating," "perplexing,"
"refreshing," and "interesting"—the last of which he says

---

[4] The following example is taken from Owen Barfield's essay, "Language, Evolution of Consciousness and the Recovery of Meaning," in
Temenos Academy Review 26 (2023): 136–44.

"is put to so many uses that we can hardly imagine how life or conversation could be carried on without it."

Pearsall Smith also observes that the adjective "interesting" appeared and became widespread in use alongside the verb "to bore," and he comments: "If we wish to enter into the state of mind of past ages, [we must] try to imagine a time when people thought more of objects than of their own emotions, and when, if they were bored or interested, they would not name their feeling, but mention the quality of object that produced it." So, for example, rather than saying "I'm bored from reading this book," one might have said, "this is a tedious book." The take-home point is that there was a time when our shared vernacular reflected little if any preoccupation with the inner self at all. As time passed, however, the inner self became the one reality around which our world and our interpretations of it were to orbit.

By the time the Second Vatican Council was convened in the 1960s, Cartesian conceptions concerning our nature and how true religion works in relation to our nature were not even defended by the fashionable theologians of the day; they were simply taken for granted, and deemed uncontroversial assumptions to be presupposed by *all* Catholic theology. The Scottish Dominican friar, Fergus Kerr, in his highly commendable work entitled *Theology After Wittgenstein*, has done a remarkable job of compiling many examples of such Cartesianism prevalent among the leading advisers of that unhappy Council.[5] He demonstrates that Cartesian dualism was indeed the house anthropology of the *nouvelle théologie*, and in turn was uncritically woven into the modern theology from which the Council developed its texts. Let me offer a few noteworthy examples.

In his *Theological Investigations*, Karl Rahner—a Jesuit—declared that there must be no going back

---

[5] See Fergus Kerr, *Theology After Wittgenstein*, second edition (London: The Society for Promoting Christian Knowledge, 1997), 7–23.

on the "anthropological turn in philosophy since Descartes."[6] Rahner's own anthropology was well conveyed in the following key passage from his *Foundations of Christian Faith*:

> A subject which knows itself to be finite...has already transcended its finiteness... Insofar as he experiences himself as conditioned and limited by sense experience, and all too much conditioned and limited, he has nevertheless already transcended this sense experience. He has posited himself as the subject of a pre-apprehension which has no intrinsic limit, because even the suspicion of such an intrinsic limitation to the subject posits this pre-apprehension itself as going beyond suspicion.[7]

No doubt that's all crystal clear. But if not, let me, as my American friends would say, "unpack it." Rahner's point is that the inner subjective self, by knowing itself, has transcended all the conditioning and limitation entailed by existing as a being in the world and the subject of the sense experience that arises from being essentially embodied. Thus, by knowing itself, such conditioning and limitation is overcome, and the unlimited, inner, *true* self is revealed to itself. Behold Karl Rahner, a faithful disciple of Descartes.

Later on, in the same work, Rahner claims that we can come to the discovery of God only through this unveiling of the inner self.[8] Hence, Rahner moves from Cartesian anthropology to Cartesian theology, following the exact same order of discovery as Descartes himself: from epistemic doubt to the finding of the self, and from the self to that on which the self is contingent. Simultaneously, Rahner puts aside the entire Aristotelian

---

[6] Karl Rahner, *Theological Investigations* (London: Darton, Longman & Todd, 1965), IX:38.
[7] Karl Rahner, *Foundations of Christian Faith* (New York: The Crossroad Publishing Company, 1978), 20.
[8] Rahner, *Foundations*, 69.

tradition of natural theological demonstration from metaphysical principles known by inference from sense experience of the actual world around us. He also puts aside the deeper Neoplatonic natural theology of emanation and participation so treasured by the Fathers, the medieval Schoolmen, and the Christian humanists of the Quattrocento. The entire Catholic philosophical tradition of natural theology is thus cast aside in favour of the inner cognitive subject and his insulated reliance on God—what *kind* of "God," we do not know.

Were such Cartesian errors just a particular obsession of Rahner, perhaps we'd be in a different situation with regard to the collapse of the Catholic intellectual tradition. But all the modernists of the mid-twentieth century were getting up to it. The philosopher Anthony Kenny points out in a review of Teilhard de Chardin's *The Phenomenon of Man* how Cartesian assumptions underpin almost every anthropological claim that Teilhard— another Jesuit, by the way—makes in that book.[9] Hans Küng declared in typically doctrinaire manner in his book *Eternal Life?*, "The history of modern epistemology from Descartes [has]...made clear that the fact of any reality at all independent of our consciousness can be accepted only in an act of trust."[10] And for Küng, our grasp of reality is not a consequence of existing as beings that emerge out of reality, who have been inducted into a didactic tradition of understanding reality. No, no. Something quite different altogether is going on, as Küng declares: "Every human being decides for himself his *fundamental attitude* to reality: that basic approach which embraces, colours, characterises his whole experience, behaviour, and action."[11]

---

[9] See Anthony Kenny, *The Legacy of Wittgenstein* (Oxford: Basil Blackwell, 1989), ch. 8.

[10] Hans Küng, *Eternal Life?: Life After Death as a Medical, Philosophical, and Theological Problem* (Eugene, OR: Wipf and Stock, 2002), 275.

[11] Hans Küng, *Does God Exist?: An Answer for Today* (Eugene, OR: Wipf and Stock, 2006), 432.

So, thanks to Küng's insights, it turns out that prior to our embodied experience, behaviour, and action in the world, there is an inner self that decides what such characteristics will be for itself. (I've never met anyone who has experienced life in this way, but there we are.) Unlike Rahner, who is a classical Cartesian in following his argument to belief in a God who is the explanation for the very existence of the thinking subject, Küng takes the original scepticism that marks the Cartesian point of departure all the way into his natural theology: "as there is no logically conclusive proof for the reality of reality, neither is there one for the reality of God."[12] Having accepted that the only reality about which we can have certainty is the existence of the cogitating subject, according to Küng, we must maintain scepticism towards everything else, including the very ground of being, namely God. (Fortunately for us, on Küng's argument we can also reasonably doubt that Hans Küng ever existed.)

But the examples roll on beyond the conciliar years. In Peter Chirico's 1977 book on papal authority, entitled *Infallibility*, we are told that "We never recognise or see another being in itself; we only recognise directly the effects of its activity towards us."[13] Rather than, as Aquinas taught, the sensible accidents conveying through our senses the true substantial form of the object of our apprehension, Chirico explains that in fact we infer some notion that there must be a unified being before us because we're subject to its effects. Presumably, in the case of another human being, the strange noises and movements that the organism before me is making indicate the presence of a spirit operating it from within.

This view of man is now very much part of the shared language of Catholic thought, conservative or not. In Timothy O'Connell's 1990 work *Principles of Catholic*

---

[12] Küng, *Does God Exist?*, 574.
[13] Peter Chirico, *Infallibility* (London: Sheed & Ward, 1977), 58.

Morality, we learn that "people might be compared to onions." (As an aside, I have long thought that many of the mistakes that arise in philosophy do so *not* necessarily due to some error in the formal structure of the reasoning from some prior and declared principle, but on account of the metaphors that we deploy, implicitly or otherwise, in making the case we're trying to develop, and as metaphors for philosophical anthropology go, bulbs and root vegetables are not good ones, in my opinion.) Having peeled away all the layers of the onion, O'Connell tells us that we find the "dimensionless pinpoint around which everything else revolves...the person himself or herself—the I."[14] In O'Connell's view, persons, then, are not disclosed to us in embodied relatedness, but rather the person is only known to himself, under layers upon layers of experience, about which he must grow in scepticism as he moves out and away from his cloistered "I." How, indeed, persons relate to one another interpersonally—or in the technical terminology of O'Connell, as *onion to onion*—remains a mystery. And one can find example after example of twentieth-century theologians committing themselves to this kind of Cartesian dualism. Fr Kerr has collated many apposite quotations for us in his marvellous book on Wittgenstein, which again I recommend to the reader.

But why is this adoption of the anthropological dualism of modernity by the Church so important and so worrying, practically speaking? Well, for a number of reasons, actually. The entire "LGBTQ+" movement—with which the Church in certain places has been flirting for some time, and to which so many of her clerical members unofficially belong—is based on the notion that there is an inner authentic self that is only accidentally related to the body. And in this view, the body's rationally apprehended telos is unable to express anything about the

---

[14] Timothy O'Connell, *Principles of Catholic Morality* (New York: Harper Collins, 1990), 59.

flourishing of the authentic self, whose purely spiritual life is—as it is with Descartes—to be privileged above whatever the body can disclose. After all, as Descartes himself put it, "I am...in the strict sense only a thing that thinks; that is, I am a mind."

Besides the moral complexities that easily arise from a commitment to Cartesian dualism, to which I have just alluded, there are other grave consequences to thinking of ourselves as "minds." One upshot of such a view is, as I've noted, that of attributing a causal power to ideas that they do not possess. Combine *that* with a privileging of the mechanistic metaphor that predominates in modernity, and ecclesiastical leadership ceases to look like shepherding or gardening—the classic metaphors for ecclesiastical leadership—and it starts to look a lot more like engineering. The engineering conception of ecclesiastical leadership found itself on steroids during the Second Vatican Council, during which a new manual for the Church's existence was developed in the form of non-dogmatic documents that were meant to lead to a new Pentecost for a new Church altogether. Out of ideas, a reality was meant to just spring to life—after all, apparently, we're all just minds, so why wouldn't things work like that? In that Council we have a clear example of what I have been describing: ideas are privileged, the entity in question—in this case, the Church herself—is analysed under the mechanistic metaphor, a manual is issued, and we've been toiling under ecclesiastical engineers ever since.

Working as a leading catechetical instructor for nearly seven years in the largest diocese in England, I was time and again baffled by the importance afforded to catechetical programmes. Almost every week, discussions were had about this or that new catechetical programme, whether we should be using "Catholic Alpha" or "Divine Renovation," or whether this or that catechetical course should be imported from Canada, the USA, or some other country, or whether this new catechetical "expert" who gets x-amount of views on YouTube should be invited over to speak in the diocese. I was repeatedly faced with the overriding assumption that the crisis of faith induction and faith retention could be solved by some new, flashy catechetical programme, when most of the Catholics whom such initiatives were meant to serve didn't even know how to pray the rosary.

Why, I used to wonder, *do my coworkers attribute to the transmission and reception of ideas a causal power which doesn't seem to exist?* For no amount of catechesis seemed to reverse the flight from the Church by her members. Recently, Prof. Stephen Bullivant has argued in his book *Mass Exodus* that the Catholic Church has, over time, come to view a devotional life as an *effect* of good catechesis, and his research challenges this very supposition. The findings of Bullivant's study reveal that attachment to the Faith—at least in the UK and the USA—was generally deepest, and most long-lasting, where catechesis was perhaps average, or even substandard, but where a very rich devotional and liturgical life, with reverently offered Masses, and also frequent vigils, litanies, processions, prayers to saints, and pilgrimages were part of the local culture.[15] The effect of such a devotional culture was a deep and stable, if not easily articulated, spiritual life in which the Faith was known and lived organically, and retention of the Faith was typically higher than in other places.

Such a view of habitual religion as causally powerful in faith retention, rather than attributing the same causal power to assent to doctrinal formulae—however important that may be—coheres well with the soteriological epistemology of St. Thomas Aquinas. Aquinas argues that the propositions of the Faith are not themselves compelling to the intellect, and thus logically prior to

---

[15] Stephen Bullivant, *Mass Exodus: Catholic Disaffiliation in Britain and America Since Vatican II* (Oxford: Oxford University Press, 2019), 102–13, 156–71.

accepting the Gospel—even if concurrently in time—God must enter the soul by means of prevenient grace and establish in the individual what Aquinas calls "a sympathy" between His own divine life and the life of the individual. Hence, for Aquinas, devotion to God wrought by God's loving communion with his creature is prior to the acceptance of doctrinal propositions, and the former has both an efficient and final causal relationship with the latter. To put that in the pithy formula of Aquinas, "the act of believing is an act of the intellect assenting to the Divine truth at the command of the will moved by the grace of God."[16] For Aquinas, then, far from being a *mind*, as Descartes claims each one of us is, we are *persons*, and we are persons insofar as we are in relation, including—nay, *especially*—in relation to God.

More importantly for my purposes, however, is that the adoption of this Cartesian anthropology has—as it is obvious it would do if wholly accepted uncritically—rendered the very notion of sacred space impossible. And *this* is the point towards which I've been creeping, and to which the final part of this chapter will be devoted, namely, how we moved from focus on the *sacred thing in the world* to focus on the *sacred idea within*—that is, how we lost the notion of sacred space. This was first brought to my attention when reading a work of Marian theology entitled *The Black Virgin*, by the French philosopher Jean Hani. In that work, amid describing his various pilgrimages to shrines of the Black Madonna around France and beyond, Hani writes the following:

> These sites often strike the least predisposed visitor with their special character, a character which is hard to define, but provokes a sense of some particularly strong 'presence.' These are sacred sites. In fact, places are not defined solely by their materiality—by 'extension,' as Descartes and his rationalist successors would have it—but more by

---

[16] *Summa Theologiae* II-II, Q. 2, art. 9, co.

> their particular 'quality,' which is dependent upon
> factors other than matter, for matter is penetrated
> by a certain irradiation of the Spirit; and there
> are privileged places where...the 'Spirit blows'
> more strongly than elsewhere.[17]

For Hani, then, it is not people having holy thoughts
or holy feelings—it is not the holiness of the supposed
interior, hidden self—that makes these sites holy, or
give us reason to speak of these sites as holy. Indeed,
Hani notes that it is often those least predisposed to
holy feelings who identify sacred places as possessing
a holy character. Nor, though, is it the mere shape or
appearance of the material place that makes it holy, or
seem holy. Instead, it is the place itself grasped under
the aspect of a category that is almost wholly neglected
today among us children of Descartes, namely the category of *quality*. The place itself, says Hani, has a certain
quality, namely the quality of the sacred. And by virtue
of this sacred quality, some places are—to use Hani's
word—"privileged" above other places, as places where
the Holy Ghost makes Himself present in a special way.

This is a topic that is extremely difficult to speak
about, precisely because the entire category of quality
has all but been lost from our purview. As the philosopher and respected Inkling Owen Barfield put it:

> Look closely and you will find there is today a
> widespread presupposition, sub-conscious for the
> most part, but raised to the level of consciousness
> in the philosophy of a value-free science, that
> there really is no such thing as quality. There is
> the useful and the useless, the desirable and the
> undesirable, and that is all.[18]

The seventeenth-century scientific revolution was
launched on the claim that a new method had emerged

---

[17] Jean Hani, *The Black Virgin: A Marian Mystery* (Kettering, OH: Angelico Press, 2016), 12–13.
[18] Barfield, "Language, Evolution of Consciousness and the Recovery of Meaning," 138.

that would not itself entertain so-called "occult qualities."
Indeed, later in the essay I just quoted, Barfield observes
that in the history of seventeenth-century philosophy, the
term "occult qualities" recurs time and again to denote
any "immaterial, and therefore imperceptible, force, or
process, or substance, or being." Thus, causes, essences,
and finalities, were at best all treated as belonging to
considerations beyond what could be known strictly
speaking, and at worst dismissed as hocus pocus. Thereafter, predicable qualities of objects were divided into
primary and secondary qualities depending on whether
they were deemed to inhere in those concrete things in
the world or instead in the mode of our perception, with
qualities like scent and colour judged to be secondary,
certainly by Shaftesbury, Locke, and their followers.

Soon, however, the perfectly rational claim was made
that non-extramental qualities were not really qualities at all but epistemic projections, and thus illusions.
The *only* realities were those unobservable, scentless,
colourless atomic foundational realities that could be
tested by experimentation and known by mathematical
formulae, and hence all ordinary qualities posited from
our everyday observations of the world were judged
illusory. Unfortunately, this meant that having chucked
out all the so-called "occult qualities," we now found
that we could say things that were really true only
when deploying the new occult language of the rising
scientific professionals. And what could be said of the
new, acceptable "occult qualities" was that they were not
qualities at all, but quantities, for the only realities were
those that could be subjected to scientific measurement.
Hence, we fell under, in the famous phrase of René
Guénon, the *reign of quantity*. Which is another way of
saying, the reduction of the world to "stuff."

Once, of course, the world is reduced to fields of atomic
and subatomic particle formations that are singularly,
structurally contiguous—that is to say, once you give up

on *things as substances*—it is difficult to see how, when this reduction is applied to oneself, one can rescue personal identity from the illusory realm of epistemic projection. The typical way of getting out of this problem is to posit another kind of occult, hidden reality called the "spiritual soul" that is deemed the one thing left that cannot be subject to scientific scrutiny—the so-called "hard problem of consciousness." Hence, the modern scientific paradigm rises and falls with anthropological dualism.

And as I say, we are all under this spell. This is evinced in my *own* use of the term "sacred space" above, for in using this term I have already conceded territory to the Cartesian colonisation of the Western mind. In truth, there is no such thing as sacred space, only sacred *places*. For a space is a measurable, quantifiable area, inter-changeable with any area of the same measurability. A space is an abstraction that exists only in a Cartesian world. Whereas sacrality is a quality, and by this qual-ity a space becomes *this* space, and hence not a space but a place. A place is *particular*, and once a given place has been sanctified, it is no longer transferable or inter-changeable with any other equivalent space—for no such space can exist. A sacred place is in the most extreme sense a place, which can be reverenced, but cannot be replaced without being desecrated.

Real estate agents often speak of kitchens or bedrooms as "useful spaces" or "comfortable spaces," and there is a simple reason for this. They do not want you to think of the place as a place, because it is not *your* place but some-one else's. If, however, they can get you to hold in your mind *this* place as an abstraction awaiting future realisa-tion according to your imaginative project for the place, you just might get excited enough to buy it. And this is why a sacred place cannot be a space: because the Lord, the Blessed Virgin, the saints, and the angels have already gathered there and made it their home, which is why sacred places must be approached with fear and trembling.

As the case of the real estate agent reveals, when concrete realities are discussed as abstractions and treated as such, it is usually because someone is trying to manipulate someone else. For this reason, ecclesiastical progressives who seek to impose their ideology on the faithful, tell us that we must "learn to change as Church." By rhetorically dropping the article "the," they linguistically turn the visible reality of *the* Church into an abstraction. The reverse is true as well, by the way, which is why the unreliable models and predictions of scientists are now referred to not as science, but *"the* science."

This error of treating ideas as more real than things has wholly infected the Church's culture. Some years ago, a documentary was made for UK television about religious life, and the presenter visited Aylesford Carmelite priory (in England's southeast), where are kept the relics of St. Simon Stock—the medieval leader of the Carmelite Order who received from Our Lady the brown scapular on the outskirts of Cambridge during a mystical apparition. In the television programme, an aging Carmelite friar explained to the presenter that St. Simon's relics themselves were not to be considered "holy"—that, he rationalised, would be superstitious. Indeed, they were just bits of bone, he explained. Their "value," the friar went on, came from the interior sense of closeness to God that people felt when visiting the relics. For this Carmelite, then, there was the inner realm where meaning could be found, and the outer realm of stuff, and the relics of St. Simon Stock were among the things to be identified as stuff.

Acceptance of the Cartesian error is now found throughout the Church's official praxis. Consider the curiously-named *Book of Blessings*, which replaced the Roman Ritual following the Second Vatican Council. On opening it, one discovers that the Church's official book of blessings is no longer in fact a book of blessings. The so-called blessings therein quickly reveal the underlying assumption of the revised text, namely that the world out there does not need to be sanctified, apparently, for only selves can be holy. Let me offer you one example from the *Book of Blessings*, the prayer for house blessings, literally a blessing to make a particular place sacred and still one of the most-used blessings among practicing Catholics:

> Lord, be close to your servants who move into this home and ask for your blessing. Be their shelter when they are at home, their companion when they are away, and their welcome guest when they return. And at last receive them into the dwelling place you have prepared for them in your Father's house, where you live for ever and ever. Amen.

Note that in the new blessing for homes, no home is blessed. This example is so typical of the entire text that a friend of mine who was involved in publishing the *Book of Blessings* refers to it as "the Book of Prayers for People in the Presence of Stuff." (Intriguingly, such a view—that neither things nor bodies nor places can be blessed, but only interior spirits—is not unprecedented; in the thirteenth-century text entitled *The Summa on the Cathars* by the ex-Cathar and Dominican, Brother Rainerius, it is stated that this belief was an explicitly declared tenet of the Albigensian, Manichaean heresy.)

By accepting the Cartesian paradigm, and dividing the world into two essential categories—the interior realm of meaning and the exterior realm of stuff—the Church has unofficially rendered the notion of sacred places impossible (for sacrality, being a species of meaning, is deemed a category of interiority alone). Many British Christians were scandalised when, in early 2024, a decision was made by the Dean of Canterbury Cathedral to turn this church, England's oldest cathedral, into a nightclub for a rave. Over two nights, drunken partygoers shook their fundaments over the hallowed ground of St. Thomas Becket's martyrdom. Of course, the precedent for such initiatives was surely set on the other side of the Tiber. The French liturgist Pierre Antoine—yet another Jesuit, and a man much admired in some quarters—said the following in the late 1960s:[19]

> We refuse to consider any place as intrinsically or ontologically sacred in itself, as this would be to localise the divine. Desacralisation has a spiritual and mystical dimension which we can scarcely ignore, and which may be perceived outside Christianity. A witness to this is one story, expressive in its crudity, taken from Buddhist literature. It is about a monk who enters a pagoda and pisses on the statue of Buddha. To a bystander who was scandalised by such a sacrilege, the monk replied simply: "Can you show me a place where I can piss without pissing on a bit of Buddheity?"

It is noteworthy that Fr Antoine's argument is so alien to the Christian way of thinking that in support of it he was forced to take a story from folk Buddhism. In any case, according to Fr Antoine, to view a church as holier than, say, a public lavatory, would be to commit the offence of localising the divine—that is, of making a space a sacred place. Whereas it is quite clear to Fr Antoine that if sacrality can found anywhere, it is to be found in the self, in the Buddheity that awaits realisation in spiritual enlightenment. Thus, Fr Antoine considers it a spiritual—even, he says, *mystical*—exercise, actively to desacralize anywhere that may be deemed sacred to the faithful.

Now, interestingly enough, seven years after Fr Antoine opined in this way, in 1974, a music festival of German electronica was hosted in Rheims Cathedral, during which inebriated young people used the confessionals and the baptistry font as urinals. So at least in Rheims Cathedral (a church dedicated to the Blessed Virgin, where the kings of France had been crowned since the

---

[19] See Geoffrey Hull, *The Banished Heart: Origins of Heteropraxis in the Catholic Church* (London: T&T Clark, 2010), 5.

ninth century), Fr Antoine's process of mystical desacralisation was complete—and exactly as he had envisaged, namely by everything being pissed on (a good general description, perhaps, of the approach to ecclesiastical management over the last half century). As an aside, I note that this sacrilegious event took place at the invitation of Archbishop Jacques Menager, who had been an important Vatican II peritus and a drafter of *Gaudium et Spes*, the principal document for opening up the Church to the modern world—well he certainly achieved *that* in his own diocese.

Now, before I get carried away with further edifying anecdotes, I wish to bring together the two conceptual points covered thus far. First, on the now dominant Cartesian anthropology that has been unofficially embraced by the Church, the only realm of meaning is the interior self. And second, that—in the words of Barfield—"there is only the useful and the useless," not the qualitative. And if these two points are brought together, it follows that a place such as Canterbury or Rheims Cathedral has any real meaning only insofar as it can be utilised in celebration of some cherished idea, given that the Cartesian paradigm dictates that meaning lies in the realm of the self and its ideas. Hence, if the greatest, most beautiful, most hope-filled idea is the idea of modernity—and the *mythos* of progress bound up with it—then these buildings are best used as quirky settings in which to celebrate that idea. And indeed, the use of a quirky setting for the celebration of modernity is a fairly good description of the vast majority of Catholic Masses over the last half-century.

Such a view, of course, has startling consequences for ecclesiastical architecture. Since churches are not holy places, but spaces where individuals gather to celebrate their inner worlds of meaning, the buildings' structure, layout, and art must reflect that purpose. Hence, a preference grows for round, comfortable, padded halls filled with abstract, faceless art—notably the kind of environment in which Rousseau's *Emile* would have freely arrived at the discovery of his authentic self.

Indeed, once the church building is considered within the Cartesian paradigm, it is difficult to see why a building is required at all. And this is exactly the message that we received during the COVID panics of 2020–22, when after 2,000 years of being told the opposite, we learned that in fact we could attend Mass while staying at home. This is baffling, because the Church has always insisted on the absolute necessity of personal presence in relation to the sacraments. One priest, however, who was too terrified during the COVID scare to visit an old dying priest and give him the Last Rites, told me: "It was alright, though, because I heard his confession over the telephone." With COVID, it seemed that the disembodification of Christianity was complete. But Christianity, unfortunately for that fearful priest, is not a disembodied religion. In fact, it teaches that grace can be received when in some places and not in others, and also by putting onto or into one's body some substances and not others. The Christian religion is embodied in the extreme, and holds that redemption incorporates material reality—including the body and all its passions—which will be fully realised at the final resurrection and the unification of heaven and earth at the Eschaton. In short, for Christians, there is no such thing as *stuff*.

Hitherto, what I have been attempting to convey is that, for complex reasons, the Church, over time, changed its conception of itself, from an institution whose mission was that of seizing literal earthly regions of Satan's principality and placing them in Christ's Kingdom, to one whose mission is the imparting of ideas and sentiments to inner selves. Thus, the Church went from a visible, liturgical, social reality to an option among ideological competitors. Indeed, Catholicism could never have degenerated into an internet genre—which is almost solely what it appears to be today—had this change of ecclesiastical self-understanding not taken place.

All of us are, I am sorry to say again, under this Cartesian spell. That is what it is to be enmeshed in modernity. I have been thinking about Cartesianism and its effects for many years now, and yet still I find that on a daily basis I have deliberately to cleanse myself of rationalist assumptions that privilege the abstract over the real, the conceptual over the concrete, the technical over the prudential, the instrumental over the true, and the internal over the relational.

The tragedy is that we are condemned to watch as this spell continues to hex the Church and deconstruct her mission of advancing a religion which in fact holds that divine revelation comes through a story, that the spiritual is known in the incarnate, that personal transformation comes through embodied relatedness (above all, relatedness with God, which is chiefly enjoyed through the corporeally present sacraments). All that is to say, by accepting Cartesianism as an unexamined foundation for what Professor Thomas Pink would call "official theology," that is, the theology of Church officials—but also for what is widely deemed contemporary orthopraxis—the institutional Church has become possessed by a spirit perfectly antithetical to its existence.

Are there any solutions to the problem that I have been sketching? I certainly do not have any ideas, programmes, or schemas for undoing what I have described. And felicitously so, given that any such proposals would perpetuate the problem, not solve it. For it is not to ideas that we ought to look for solutions, but to practices and places. Happily, the traditional movement of the Catholic Church is doing precisely this, quite intuitively. It is noteworthy that the Chartres pilgrimage grows each year, with numbers of pilgrims going from 12,000 in 2022 to 16,000 in 2023, to well over 18,000 in 2024, all travelling to what is surely one of the most sacred places in Europe.[20]

If we can only find liberation, just partially, from the Cartesian spell, the sacrality of place begins to reveal itself. In one of the hagiographies of St. Neot—an English saint of the ninth century—we read that near to where the saint lived in the deep woods, there was "an angel who loved to hover in hallowed places, and to breathe the air which was sanctified by the devotions of God's saints." This was the world that our ancestors inhabited. They beheld a landscape covered in sacred glades and groves consecrated by the rituals of holy men and women, wherein potent spirits delighted in dwelling.

One springtide, I was hiking in the Cotswolds with my father, and we stopped to rest by a shallow pool within a small woodland. The peacefulness and other-worldliness of that place were remarkable, as if angels loved that place and were gathering there between the trees around us. Later I learned that the pool is called St. Edward's well, for England's sainted king had performed a miracle there, back in the eleventh century, when he was visiting the poor in the area. I hadn't actually been imagining the angels at all.

I dare say we must rediscover our liturgy as a baptised form of "theurgy," a term largely gone from Christian theology today, but one that was repeatedly deployed to discuss Christian worship by such an eminent authority as St. Dionysius the Areopagite.[21] By Christian theurgy, I mean the fulfilment of all religious sacrifice, during which those offering the sacrifice commune with the divine spirits and call God down into

---

[20] The holiness and mysteriousness of Chartres Cathedral, whose Black Madonna provided the philosopher Jean Hani with a lifetime of contemplation, is well known to readers of Fulcanelli, and more recently to those interested in the work of the sacred geometer Keith Critchlow.

[21] See Kjetil Kringlebotten, *Liturgy, Theurgy, and Active Participation: On Theurgic Participation in God* (Eugene, OR: Cascade Books, 2023), 108.

the inner chamber as they chant the sacred words and perform the sacred rituals.

Like the theurgic practitioners of the Mediterranean, many early Christians, following their liturgies, would practise incubation. They would enter a deep sleep through which the sacrality of the place, now sanctified by God's sacrifice, would operate on them as they wandered in the dream world. The dream world is given extreme importance throughout the Bible as a realm in which God speaks to man, and this is especially the case in the New Testament, and yet it is a realm which is wholly neglected by modern, rationalistic Christianity. The practice of incubation was contingent on an acknowledgement of the power of sacred places to bring us into states of consciousness in which God, through His saints and angels, can draw very close to us. Johannes Trithemius, the fifteenth-century German Benedictine abbot of Sponheim, wrote two books on the practice of incubation, but those works are neglected by Christians today.[22] Incidentally, I once asked Bishop Erik Varden, previously Abbot of the English Trappist Monastery of Mount St. Bernard and now the Bishop of Trondheim in Norway, what he thought of the practice of Christian incubation. He replied, "That is indeed the purpose of the monastery guesthouse, for any seasoned guestmaster can tell you what a powerful change people can undergo merely by sleeping in a place sanctified by the Holy Mass and the chanting of the Psalms."

In sum, I propose that we return the beating heart of Christ to His Mystical Body by expelling rationalism—what I have called the Cartesian spell—from the institutional Church. Only this, I submit, will allow us to recover once more the transforming power of true religion, which is at once both profoundly mysterious and gloriously incarnational.

---

[22] See Frater Acher, *Black Abbot, White Magic: Johannes Trithemius and the Angelic Mind* (n.p.: Scarlet Imprint, 2020), 11–72.

2

MYSTICISM AS THE FOUNDATION OF PHILOSOPHY

I T is not uncommon among intellectual conservatives, especially those who are my Catholic coreligionists, to disparage René Descartes for having ruptured the Western mind and sent it on a course that has ultimately led to all the solipsism, ugliness, and despair of modernity. No doubt there is much truth in this account and I myself enjoy taking swings at Descartes, as demonstrated by the previous chapter. Nonetheless, that lazy and conceited Frenchman raised a philosophical question which is perfectly legitimate, though I wish it had never been asked: is it possible for my senses to convey to my mind an object that is not in fact there? In other words, can I see a flower, pick it, smell its fragrance, and be convinced that it is truly a flower and that it truly exists, and for nothing to be there at all?

Descartes gives various examples of how such an epistemic error might occur, including the fact of dreams and hallucinations as well as his famous thought experiment involving an evil demon that places misleading or false apprehensions in the mind. We must concede that these examples do at least indicate that it is possible in principle both to judge that something exists and to judge what it is that exists, and for the thing in question not to exist at all. And if that is possible, presumably it is also possible for *all* my "sense-data" to comprise such cases—at least in principle. Indeed, the fundamental premise on which the entire story of *The Matrix* movies is based imagines this exact notion.

Of course, someone in the classical realist (that is, broadly, the premodern) tradition will want to say: if

it is possible—and we know it *is*, at least in principle—
for the senses to be unreliable conduits of reality, then
cases in which they *are* unreliable depart from the norm.
The senses, he will say, truly convey to me the external
world—albeit imperfectly, in a limited way, and distorted
by all sorts of assumptions about the world unique to
me and my conditioning. But the essences which are
conveyed by the attributes of things, transmitted via my
sense data, which I grasp by my mind's eye, really do
correspond to the things out there in the world. And the
judgement of existence that I make on such things, to
say that they truly do exist, corresponds to the being of
the things out there in the world. And if there is an error
in my apprehension of the world, that is not because
there is a problem with the way the world is constituted
or with the way that I am constituted *per se*, nor with
how I relate to the world, but because something has
in this particular instance gone terribly wrong. If this
account were not the case, the classical realist would
say, we could not discuss the topic at all.

Such a response from such a classical realist philosopher may be reasonable, but it does not get us out
of the Cartesian problem. After all, what justifies the
assumption that his misapprehension of reality is *in this
instance* a departure from the norm? Is it because he can
make a distinction between hallucination and proper
judgement, dreaming and being awake, being free from
demonic possession and being fettered by it? *But what
if*, the Cartesian will respond, *all these distinctions merely
distinguish between different aspects of unreality?*

Up until Descartes, philosophers had taken it as a
given that one's philosophising ought to begin with
thinking about the reality that we encounter in the world,
and that by so doing we ought to try to make sense of
it. It simply never occurred to philosophers before the
1630s to begin their philosophising with considerations
about the operations of the mind. Classical philosophers

uncritically—perhaps unthinkingly—maintained a relative confidence in their senses as reliable conduits of
data about the world around them, as conveying the
attributes and in turn the *forms* of the things in the
world. Thus, they trusted in their minds' comprehension
of the natures or essences of things, and in their ability
to judge correctly what things did or did not exist, insofar as they had the apposite experience to make such
judgements. And the reason they wandered about with
this general confidence in their own ability to grasp
reality was that they were—generally speaking—mystics,
and those who were not mystics but physicalists (and
there were a few of those among the pre-Socratics) were
formed within a mystical culture.[1]

Anaximander with his account of the eternal Apeiron,
Heraclitus and his Logos of perennial fire, Pythagoras
and his ascetic path to union with the perfect harmony
underpinning all mathematical and musical order—the
superstructure, if you like, of the cosmos—all these
men were mystical writers. Thanks to the work of Peter
Kingsley, people have become more aware of the mystical lifeblood of the Western philosophical tradition,
especially that found in Parmenides and Empedocles,
Kingsley's own especial teachers, who were indeed religious poets conveying mystical insights. Plato, of course,
believed that spiritual ascent to the realm of uncreated
and perfect forms was the purpose of the philosophical life, and Aristotle held that the culmination of all
practical wisdom was the contemplation of God as He
contemplates His own perfection.

---

[1] Admittedly, there was a philosophical tradition of scepticism in the
ancient world. Perhaps the most famous pre-Socratic Greek sceptic was
Gorgias, whose scepticism was presented in the work *On Non-Existence*.
Later, so-called "Academic Scepticism" dominated Plato's Academy
following the founder's death. This tradition of scepticism is not,
though, my concern; for it does not belong to the realist tradition
that Christian civilisation made its own, and it largely vanished from
the Western world until the late Middle Ages, when it emerged to
assist the process of undoing that civilisation.

This understanding of philosophy as a pathway of mysticism was at the heart of the Neoplatonic project. Plotinus, seeing everything as both a participation in, and emanation of, the One, embarked on a life of remarkable asceticism in pursuit of perfect spiritual union with the Absolute, due to which he would often enter states of ecstasy for many hours. His followers never departed from his conception of philosophy, and whilst Neoplatonism largely competed against Christianity in the Church's early centuries, the latter soon baptised the fundamental insights of Neoplatonism, making its metaphysics the vital framework within which Patristic theology developed.

The mystical assumption at the heart of philosophy, which I believe delayed any asking of the Cartesian question for so many centuries, is that the world is in some mysterious way a divine communication. The world is a heavenly declaration to that part of it that possesses the requisite rational faculties to receive it— namely, us. The foundation of any realist philosophy, then, is essentially religious. To the modern mind, cut off as it is from any overarching mystical worldview, there could not be a weaker foundation on which to build a philosophical account of reality; to the classical mind, however, it is the strongest foundation on which to embark on the philosophical life, which is not merely a game of conceptual conjoinings, but a pathway leading to personal transformation in ultimate reality.[2]

That the philosophical endeavour rests on a religious foundation ought not to trouble us if we have already accepted an inextinguishable fact about our own human nature, namely that we must, and will, worship. Without this assumption—which does not lend itself to demonstration beyond noting the historical fact that man has, as long as man has been, ever worshipped rightly or

---

[2] See Peter Kwasniewski, "Ecstasy and the Love of Wisdom," *The European Conservative*, April 14, 2024.

worshipped idolatrously, but never not worshipped—no philosophy, and indeed no life of the mind at all, is safe. Without some prior wonder at creation as the declaration of its Author, and therefore as an intelligible reality that corresponds to minds because it is a product of Mind, all philosophy collapses into scepticism. Even the most basic scientific research is impossible unless the scientist believes in such a correspondence of his mind to reality (but few scientists, and none of the most ardent secular ones, ask themselves *why* they should assume that this is so). Without the mystical intuition, the intellect enters an inescapable spiral of anxiety-ridden, self-directed nitpicking. The childlike wonder at the world which underpins the philosophical life corrupts into the childish confusion that underpins modernity.

On a personal note, it is because I have always understood the philosophical life to rest on a religious intuition that it has ever seemed not only reasonable but necessary to combine philosophy with spiritual practices and physical exercises. Far from eccentric, before modernity there was not a single philosopher worthy of the name who did not think the same. And given that my whole life is marked by an attempt to cultivate a premodern mind, it shouldn't surprise my readers that this is how I approach the discipline. The threefold way of corresponding oneself to reality, namely that of the temple, the academy, and the gymnasium, has always belonged to our civilisation as the three-pillared arcade on whose sacred ground Sophia abides. But take the mystical out from underneath those pillars—that is, remove the sacred ground—and the whole structure crumbles. We exist, ultimately, for union with God, and philosophy as much as any other aspect of a cultivated human life must acknowledge that, or it becomes a mere spectre of itself and ruinous to those it is meant to serve.

3

ACKNOWLEDGING THE CRISIS AND
BREAKING THE SPELL

E ARLIER, I gave the theologian Karl Rahner a
hard time, and indeed he may have done more
to undermine the integrity of Catholic orthodoxy
at the higher levels of theological scholarship than
any other member of modern theology's cognoscenti.
Though it's difficult to say who deserves that particular
accolade, as the twentieth century provided so much
competition. Be that as it may, Rahner famously made
a remark with which I have found myself in increasing
agreement as time rolls on and the decay of the institutional Church is ever more evident: "The Christian
of the future will be a mystic or will not exist at all."

Now, whatever Rahner *meant* by this sentence I'd
likely deem anathema. Taken in isolation, however,
this proposition seems to point a way forward in an
otherwise impossible situation. The situation to which
I refer is what I've been calling for some time now
the Church's "post-authority epoch." When I say this,
I predominantly have in mind the Catholic Church
(being, as I am, a Roman Catholic). The ugly internal power games, moral relativising, and neocaesa-
ropapism of Orthodox senior clerics, however, have
hugely undermined the authority of their offices as
well, and it's not even worth remarking on the state
of the Anglican Communion and the various Protestant sects. The fact is, *all* the baptised are in the
same boat when it comes to the current crisis: the
institution that the Incarnate Word established on
earth to lead "all nations" to "all truth" has lost its
authority (Matthew 28:19, John 16:13).

Recently, I picked up my copy of Pope John Paul II's *Veritatis Splendor* to refresh my memory with respect to his arguments for the reality of intrinsic evils. Whilst I hold that moral thinking requires serious engagement with intentions, conditions, and circumstances, I reject "situation ethics"; morality *per se* clearly liquefies once you deny that some acts are forbidden regardless of circumstances. But I wanted to analyse the arguments advanced by John Paul II against situation ethics, and to my shock I found that he advances no arguments. He simply says that both Scripture and Church tradition hold that some acts are always and everywhere forbidden, and that this is *his* teaching as Vicar of Christ. That three decades ago it was still possible for a pope to make claims on the weight of his authority amazed me. This would be impossible today; the papal office simply doesn't possess the existential authority for such confident assertions anymore.

Since the late nineteenth century, the faithful have been subjected to ever more regular, and ever longer, papal encyclicals and exhortations. Under the pontificate of Pope Francis, these have taken the form of very long essays, mostly comprising observations and occasional hints at the revolutionary direction behind their authorship. It is almost as if Pope Francis is begging to be taken seriously by the faithful for a moment, as he feigns speaking to them on an equal footing. This, though, is not at all how he has actually *governed* the Church, bypassing canon law and settled theology as he pleases, and persecuting those members of the faithful who won't, so to speak, get with the programme. This, of course, is exactly what belongs to the psychology of an abusive man: he oscillates from begging to be loved and listened to, to throwing his fists around. A central reason why abusive people behave in this way is because they have lost authority. They can no longer be believed or trusted, and so they resort to begging, sentimental gestures, and then violence.

The hierarchy of the Church has almost entirely lost authority in the eyes of the rest of the faithful. This isn't a speculative deduction offered in some attempt to explain the phenomena. What I am describing is the situation as it is—a matter of fact. Among the vocal, active Catholics of the second half of the twentieth century, there were broadly three factions: the progressives, the traditionalists, and the post-conciliar neocons. That third category was dominant until the reign of Pope Francis, but since then has nearly totally disappeared. The champions of the "hermeneutic of continuity" have, generally speaking, fallen silent. It was too difficult to keep it up. Francis amply demonstrated that the post-conciliar age is an age of ecclesiastical and theological rupture, and to argue that this isn't the case became impossible. The neocons tried to maintain their position for the first five years of Francis's papacy, attempting to render orthodox every one of his bizarre allocutions, but in the end, it just became too tiring and too embarrassing.

Thereafter, among vocal, active Catholics, there remained two dominant groups: the progressives and the traditionalists. Neither of these groups maintained much confidence in the authority of the Holy See or the curia. The progressives never believed that the law of the Church, the dogmas of the Faith, or the moral law had any claim on their intellect or conscience in any case, beyond what they individually chose to accept. The trads always believed they were bound by such things, but see now that something's happened to the Church's government that makes it no longer trustworthy, and thus they look sideways at anything coming out of Rome. Under Francis, the progressives have been happy to affirm the Church's authority, but only because it served their ideology to do so; they were certainly more reluctant under John Paul II and Benedict XVI. What this means is that neither of the two dominant groups of vocal, active Catholics trusts the hierarchy's authority merely on the grounds that it belongs to the government of a divine institution. Thus, the Church is, as a matter of fact, in a post-authority epoch.

Catholics who believe what Catholics have always believed, and wish to worship as Catholics have always worshipped, seemingly find themselves judged as heterodox in the contemporary Church supposedly born from the "new Pentecost" of the Second Vatican Council. Remarkably, as devotional life corroded under the liturgical experiments following that Council, and the popular piety of the laity was belittled, Catholic dioceses responded to this spiritual asphyxia by increasingly reframing the Faith as a purely catechetical enterprise—with or without orthodox teaching. At the very moment, then, when the teaching authority of the hierarchy was precisely what was being called into question, and at the very moment when the Holy Father wouldn't stop tampering with the *Catechism of the Catholic Church* (so that it now teaches what was condemned as heresy in previous ages), the hierarchy emphasised its role as Teacher. Few, of course, were convinced. The problem, too, goes all the way down: Catholics are just as suspicious of the teachings from their parish pulpits as they are towards the stuff coming out of Rome.

Meanwhile, the Church from its highest echelons to the local diocese has been riddled with petty clericalism, law-breaking, sexual abuse, and general moral and financial corruption. Anyone who follows Catholic journalism will be well aware of the depth of the rot. For a long time, many members of the Catholic clergy have been practising homosexuals who could not in good conscience preach the Faith, and so largely limited themselves to managing ecclesiastical decline—and were often content to say as much. They knew they had lost any defensible authority before their own flocks, and this caused them immense frustration. Many a Catholic has had the experience of disagreeing on some minor point with a cleric and immediately finding himself confronted by an enraged, red-faced cartoon character, pointing and frothing at the mouth. As one priest—one of the few good ones—said to me, "it seems to be something they pick up at seminary."

When I was in my early thirties, I challenged a bishop over what I judged to be his breaking of employment law and violation of Catholic social doctrine. A priest soon wrote to me, expressing his horror at my lack of "caution" in challenging the "Lord's anointed." Interestingly, this priest didn't tell me that I was *wrong*, only that the bishop shouldn't be challenged—seemingly on no other grounds than that he was a bishop. To think it is appropriate to use language suitable for an authority that has manifestly been lost indicates how delusional these clerics truly are. This attitude is typical of the servile—rather than filial—obedience that has taken over the Church's hierarchy. Indeed, without such widespread servile obedience, the hierarchy would never have been able to perpetuate so many unspeakable evils for which it is now universally infamous. The reason, of course, that so many clerics behaved in this bizarre way—and continue to do so—is precisely because clerical authority is gone, and they have been trying to keep the illusion of its existence going for as long as possible.

That the Church's ministers are managing decline and have capitulated to the post-Christian world at every step is an open secret. During the COVID pandemonium, the Church's bishops closed the churches. The Bishops of England and Wales preemptively begged the government to authorise the closure of their churches before the government had even proposed such measures. Pope Francis decreed that taking an experimental drug of malign origin was an "act of love," and in violation of Church teaching he threatened Vatican employees with loss of employment if they failed to undergo the procedure. The hierarchy effectively proclaimed that, at a time of widespread alarm and instability, the Church's ministers wished to abandon the faithful. Worse still, the hierarchy would help to foment the draconian measures, power-grabbing, and destruction of civil liberties by state governments. For the first time in the Church's history, the Apostles' successors apocalyptically cancelled the festive liturgies of the Easter Octave. The Church's teachers in effect declared that sanctifying the faithful, preaching the Gospel, and making disciples of all nations did not constitute "essential services." If the Church was not fully in the post-authority epoch before all that, it certainly was by the time we were coming out of the lockdown tyranny. And many of the faithful, quite understandably, have never come back to Mass.

Tolkienians will understand the overriding mentality of the clergy. I call it the "Denethor mentality," after the Steward of Gondor in *The Lord of the Rings*. A man desperately holding onto power, whose behaviour and form of government is becoming increasingly erratic and self-serving, who cannot see what is required amid a crisis, who concedes ever more territory to the powers that want to destroy his realm, who rejects that on which his authority rests, and who rewards foolishness whilst seeking every opportunity to crush his only remaining, faithful, and devoted son. *That* is Denethor mentality, and it has become the dominant mentality of the Catholic clergy.

Since the late medieval period, every form of check and balance in the Church has incrementally diminished. The influence of the temporal power of the Church, namely the laity, on ecclesiastical matters has so ebbed that the laity now has no influence whatever. The clerical hierarchy—especially the pope—is now totally unchecked. If the pope has an idea, he can type it up on a piece of paper, put his name at the bottom of it, and suddenly that becomes *law*. And that is exactly how Pope Francis has governed the Church. The situation is ridiculous and, again, has corroded to the point of destroying the last residue of authority in the Church.

In the so-called age of ecclesiastical collegiality, there is zero collegiality. The whole thing is a smokescreening exercise. Attempting to make sense of this situation, the faithful have increasingly fallen back on the *sensus fidelium* to "tap into," so to speak, the *true* faith of the ages that is being covered up with recurrent acts of clerical voluntarism. The Church's government knows that this is what has happened, and thus diabolically sought to imitate the *sensus fidelium* through Francis's "synodal process," so that it appeared that the "sense of the faithful" conveniently affirmed the revolutionary direction of the governing clergy.

Over the last century, the Catholic Church has undergone the greatest apostasy in its history. And yet, amazingly, people *are* still sporadically converting to Catholicism. In the West, such people—especially young people—are coming to the Catholic Church through the traditional liturgy and the wider traditionalist movement. Indeed, a strange characteristic of the post-authority epoch is that the parish and the diocese aren't really where Catholicism happens. Catholicism has largely become an internet genre. And whilst the Church's government is doing all it can, from the very top, to destroy the traditionalist movement, that movement certainly remains alive and well online. It is mainly by this virtual world that young people come to Catholicism in their attempt to escape the Manichaeism and nihilism of late modernity (which mainstream Catholicism only appears to offer in ceremonial form). On arrival into the fold, however, such young people soon find that their new spiritual fathers wish they had never become Catholics. Having escaped the world that tried to ruin their souls, they find themselves in a Church that officially wishes they'd never existed.

The Church's greatest modern theologians have been committed to explaining to us that nature is in fact supernature (à la Teilhard de Chardin), the difference between a Christian and a non-Christian is one of degree rather than of kind (à la Karl Rahner), and that everyone is going to be saved from damnation in any case (à la Hans Urs von Balthasar). Then *Dignitatis Humanae*—Vatican II's Declaration on Religious Freedom—came along and seemingly cancelled the Church's mission to the temporal world. By the end of modern theology's process of conflating the natural and supernatural, dissolving them into one another in a perverse act of theological alchemy, Catholics were left asking: what is the point?

It is not as if being a committed Christian doesn't entail some serious challenges in a world that is increasingly hostile to such a life. If it turns out that certain sins cannot in fact be resisted, and therefore giving into them cannot be blamed on you, as Pope Francis implied;[1] that there's no real difference between being baptised and being unbaptised; that venerating saints and worshipping Amazonian fertility gods is really all the same;[2] that the Church isn't actually charged with making disciples of all nations because religious pluralism is willed by God;[3] and that everyone is going to be saved anyway, Catholics may reasonably feel that it's preferable to throw in the towel altogether—and so they have.

The concordat with the post-Christian world, which is the overarching theme of the post-conciliar settlement, also implies that there's no lay apostolate. Traditionally, the role of the clergy was to sanctify the laity, that the laity may sanctify the world, capturing it from the

[1] For a comprehensive analysis of the many statements and actions of Pope Francis that undermine traditional moral teaching, see John R.T. Lamont and Claudio Pierantoni, *Defending the Faith against Present Heresies* (Waterloo, ON: Arouca Press, n.d. [2021]).
[2] See Gavin Ashenden, "Why Pachamamas have no place in the Church," *The Catholic Herald* online, May 25, 2023, https://catholicherald.co.uk/why-pachamamas-have-no-place-in-the-church/.
[3] See Edward Pentin, "Does the New Catholic-Muslim Declaration Deviate from Catholic Teaching?," *National Catholic Register* online, February 15, 2019, www.ncregister.com/news/does-the-new-catholic-muslim-declaration-deviate-from-catholic-teaching.

"prince of this world" and placing it under the Kingship of Christ. Were this apostolate of the laity to continue, however, it would seriously undermine the Church's new concordat with the unconverted world, implying that there was some substantial difference between a sacralised world and a profane one, which would some-what undo the nature-supernature conflation on which the Vatican II theology of "opening up to the world" was indeed based.[4] So, what is the laity to do in the modern Church? Carry the cruets up to the altar and join the parish folk band, I suppose. The laity may be forgiven for saying, *thanks but we have more important things to do with our time.*

I have barely touched upon the crisis. I've mentioned just *some* of the problems faced by the Church in its post-authority epoch, because for now I only want to draw the attention of my readers to the fact that there *is* a crisis. And this crisis has moved the Church into a new mode of existence: the Church's government has lost its authority, and the faithful should not only expect an intensification of mistreatment by arbitrary power from the hierarchy, as the hierarchy fails to come to terms with this reality, but the faithful will also need to work out what it practically means to be a faithful Christian in this new epoch.

Many today, looking around at the spiritual wasteland that is the West, seek to satiate their deepest religious thirsts by turning to romantic ideas of pre-Christian paganism, nature-worship, and New Age spirituality. Otherwise, they look east to the mysticisms of Asia, especially those of Buddhism and Hinduism, both of which have the added advantage of easily accommo-dating the individualism, solipsism, and anthropological

---

[4] See Thomas Pink, "Vatican II and Crisis in the Theology of Bap-tism," in Edmund Waldstein, O. Cist., *Integralism and the Common Good: Selected Essays from* The Josias, vol. 2: The Two Powers (Brooklyn, NY: Angelico Press, 2022), 290–334.

dualism which have colonised the Western mind since
the so-called Enlightenment. I threw myself into all
these spiritualities, in fact—a sequence that culminated
in my conversion to Catholic Christianity on the south
coast of India in early adulthood, and I'm certain that
God drew me out of the West that I might encounter
His Church beyond its visibly corrupt and decadent
occidental condition.

In *Crossing the Threshold of Hope*, John Paul II spec-
ulated that many Westerners had turned especially to
Buddhism because the practices of Carmelite spirituality hadn't been properly disseminated among the
faithful. Had they been taught such practices, he suggested, people would have seen that whatever they were
looking for in Eastern mysticism was already present
in the Christian spiritual tradition.[5] Now, I've read
John of the Cross, Teresa of Avila, Brother Lawrence
of the Resurrection, and Edith Stein. Carmelite spirituality, which I deeply admire, is a very ascetical—
almost eremitical—spirituality, and it's difficult to see
how it is applicable to life in the world. Admittedly,
this gap was somewhat bridged by Thérèse of Lisieux's
autobiography, which hugely influenced lay spirituality.
Nonetheless, it doesn't seem sufficient to tell religiously
hungry Westerners that they need not look to the East,
as they can just read John of the Cross and thereby
create for themselves an oasis in the spiritual desert
that is the Church's post-conciliar condition.

We must spiritually engage with the situation at hand.
As the West continues to plummet into its now unavoidable civilisational collapse, we shall see the rise of all
kinds of superstitions and witchcrafts, which will likely
serve to bestow a religious character upon the techno-
cratic age of bio-government and transhumanism that
we've now entered. The Church's hierarchy has not only

---

[5] See John Paul II, *Crossing the Threshold of Hope* (London: Random
House, 1994), 86–90.

shown every sign of celebrating this diabolic trajectory, which it doesn't even begin to understand, but even if it became critical of it, it remains completely unequipped to engage with the new global regime in the prophetic way that's desperately needed. Those who see that we're in for something quite different from the interminable capital-P "Progress" that liberalism promised to deliver are increasingly looking for a spiritual awakening that will reconcile us to God and to His creation that we've defaced, and the institutional Church stands at the sidelines looking baffled at such people.

The West is entrenched in what the philosopher and psychologist John Vervaeke has called a "meaning crisis"; whilst the institutional Church has entered an authority crisis. I submit that the Church's reclaiming of its mission is the only way out of the meaning crisis of the West—a crisis that the West has successfully exported to almost every part of the globe—and at present the Church remains utterly unfit to take up this mission. Restoring any kind of credibility will not be the work of decades, but of centuries. By then, it may be too late. So, in the meantime, I suggest that the Church has before it the imperative to rediscover its role not primarily as an authority that makes truth-claims by which to bind the intellect and the conscience of its members, but as the *path*—"the Way," as the early Christians called their religion—to encounter the God who is Love, through the mediation of Christ's sacred humanity, in a profound and transformative mystical life.

In the current situation, it seems that the remaining Church's faithful will persevere by opting to double down on the devotional life. This is exactly what all the committed Christians I know are doing. They're taking stock of the collapse of our civilization and the utter sterility of the institutional Church in the face of it, and in response they're deepening their spiritual lives and clinging to Christ. The reason for which the Church exists is the union of its members with the Triune God. And when the hierarchy's members forget this in their pursuit of worldly ambitions, God's people must consider what lies within their own spiritual repertoire and mine those resources to cultivate as far as possible the richest interpersonal relationship with Jesus Christ that they can; or better, that *He* can cultivate in them.

It seems to me that the paradigm of rationalism—with all its chaotic relationships, ugly architecture, shallow sentimentalism, fetishization of abstractions, legal positivism, and blindness to persons—to which the institutional Church has conceded so much moral territory, must be overcome if we are to recover the primacy of the mystical in the life of the Church. The challenge before us, then, is that of recapturing the theocentrism on which our civilisation was built. The Gospel, which the Church is meant to proclaim, is the means by which to do that, and the sacraments possess the power to effect the transformation that's needed. Breaking out of the prevailing rationalist paradigm, however, is the fundamental precondition for recovering the theocentric paradigm that is its antithesis. And such a deliverance may mean that we will have to be more open to a broader Western spiritual tradition which has always been bound up with mainstream Christian spirituality, but which cannot be accommodated by the rationalist paradigm and thus has been eclipsed in recent times.

What I'm pointing to is the imperative to re-enchant our world, and in turn encounter the God whose emanated likeness it is. The onset of civilizational disenchantment was already being flagged at the end of the eighteenth century by the man of letters Friedrich Schiller, whose insights on this theme were taken up a century later by the sociologist Max Weber as he analysed the bureaucratisation of society in the modern age and its corollary, the reduction of atomised individuals to—as he put it—"cogs in a machine." The pressing imperative to re-enchant our world, then, has long been acknowledged. I want to suggest that it may require a courageous recovery of the mystical, supranatural, Neoplatonic vision that comprised the fundamental superstructure on which the Patristic, Medieval, and Renaissance projects were built—a vision that has been so alien to us since the dawn of modernity.

There is clearly enormous appetite for such an enchanted vision, as demonstrated not only by the turn of Westerners to the mysticisms of the East, but by the return of theories concerning a "world-soul" and "living nature" throughout the Western academy in the form of the latest scholarly superstition: physicalist panpsychism. These are all feeble attempts to respond to the fundamental challenge that the West faces, and the Church is the only institution that possesses the supernatural power to respond properly. But to respond thus, the Church, in the titanic task of unshackling itself from the modern paradigm, may have to offer a chair at its table to Hermes Trismegistus, perhaps next to Plato, Aristotle, Cicero, Seneca, and so many other greats whom it has retrospectively baptised.

4

BEHOLD, THE KINGDOM OF GOD IS WITHIN YOU

I ARGUED in the last chapter that the Church has entered what I call its post-authority epoch. As Christians have accepted that they must treat the Church's authoritative offices with ever more suspicion, they've asked themselves—tacitly or otherwise—what it means to "follow the Lamb wherever He goes" in an institution that is largely repudiating His mission (Apocalypse 14:4). In response, many have intensified their personal devotional lives and focused on cultivating the habits of intimacy with God. As this progressively becomes the only option, Christians—I have suggested—will likely need to be more open to a broader spiritual tradition which has been at home in the Church sometimes less and sometimes more, depending on the era.

In the early 1460s, Marsilio Ficino, one of the greatest minds of the Italian Renaissance, was working on the newly rediscovered Platonic dialogues (brought to the West during the Council of Florence, which incidentally achieved the reunification of Catholics and Orthodox for half a century) and he was beginning to write his comprehensive commentary on these dialogues under the patronage of Lorenzo de' Medici. Then, unexpectedly, he was given a Greek copy of the *Corpus Hermeticum* of Hermes Trismegistus—the central mystery text of esoteric transformation. Ficino immediately stopped his work to focus all his efforts on translating it into Latin. What Ficino soon realised was that out of the Hermetic traditions, along with those of Platonism and Neoplatonism, emerged a metaphysical language expressive of the vertical vision of the cosmos common to all religious traditions. From this Ficino derived a notion, later developed by his brilliant student Giovanni Pico della Mirandola: the *prisca theologia*—the ancient theology that underpins all natural religion, which is illumined and transfigured by the renewing power of grace that belongs to supernatural religion.

The vertical vision of reality that lies at the heart of the *prisca theologia*, which has all but vanished from the purview of the Western mind due to the spells— curses, in fact—of rationalism and materialism, also constitutes the fundamental ontological structure on which Thomas Aquinas erected his theology two centuries before Ficino began his work. (Perhaps this is unsurprising, given that Aquinas's teacher, the Doctor of the Church Albert the Great, was a dedicated Hermeticist and astrologer.)

For Aquinas, the universe is made up of individuals, and yet those individuals possess a universality by their logical participation in species classes and genera. So, each individual being has an essence which it shares with other beings. Such things share essences because they participate in a logical likeness (species and genus) in the divine mind, and they exist as *individuals* because they participate in a likeness of an idea of them as individuals in the divine mind. Put simply: I exist because God thinks of me. But I also exist because God, having created an essence of me from the exemplar idea of me in His mind, has held that created essence together with an "act of existence" in a single substance (that I call myself). In sum: I exist because God thinks of me and *wills* that I exist.

The take-home lesson of this metaphysical digression is that, for Aquinas, everything that exists reflects God inasmuch as it reflects an idea in His mind, and also everything reflects God by having existence, thereby reflecting Him who *is* existence. This is Aquinas's theory of the dual exemplarism of creation. The universe, then, for Aquinas, is one great "Icon of God."[1] When an iconographer dies, however, that doesn't entail the destruction of the icon; but according to Aquinas, were God to stop thinking of the universe for one instant, the whole thing would vanish. Thus, the relation of creation to the Creator is perhaps more like the relation of song to singer. J. R. R. Tolkien, in fact, captured this notion in his "Ainulindalë" creation account in *The Silmarillion*, wherein angelic co-creators produce a music of essences taught to them by the Creator, to which the Creator grants existence, and out of the celestial chorus the material cosmos unfolds.[2]

The Neoplatonic ontology of Aquinas was generally neglected by the Catholic seminary manualists of the last few centuries, bewitched as so many were with the assumptions of rationalism. For natural theology, such writers preferred to focus on the famous Five Ways, to which Aquinas devoted one article of the *Summa Theologiae*, and they largely ignored the deeper ontology that undergirded the other 2,668 articles of that work. Thankfully, due to the efforts of the so-called "existential Thomist school"—with figures such as Cornelio Fabro, Louis-Bertrand Geiger, and W. Norris Clarke, and more recent scholars like John F. Wippel and Gregory T. Doolan—a felicitous recovery of this ontology is taking place.

Fabro himself noted that a century or so before the hex of rationalism ensorcelled the Western mind, Ficino—as a proto-existential Thomist—had been tracing this Neoplatonic ontology in the writings of Aquinas:

> One philosopher who was decidedly on his way to seeing in Thomas the metaphysical tension... grounded in the notion of participation, was Marsilio Ficino, the prince of Humanism of the

---

[1] For an extended analysis of Aquinas's participation metaphysics, see my work *The World as God's Icon: Creator and Creation in the Platonic Thought of Thomas Aquinas* (Brooklyn, NY: Angelico Press, 2020).

[2] See J. R. R. Tolkien, *The Silmarillion* (London: Book Club Associates, 1978), 15–23; cf. Jonathan S. McIntosh, *The Flame Imperishable: Tolkien, St. Thomas, and the Metaphysics of Faerie* (Kettering, OH: Angelico Press, 2017).

Quattrocento. In his major work, the *Theologica Platonica*, he acknowledges the principal theses of Thomistic metaphysics and, while recalling the notion of participation, he fights against the triumphant Averroism with the same arguments used by St. Thomas, whom he calls "the bright light of Christian theology." Had his voice been heard, many useless disputes within the orders would have been avoided.[3]

I want to suggest that the Church is now stuck in a rut, and consequently is unable to respond both to its own crisis of authority and to the overshadowing of meaning in the West. We waste time on "useless disputes," to pick up Fabro's words, rather than breaking out of the paradigm that has entrenched us in this double crisis in the first place. In the High Renaissance, when the writing of the scientific revolution was on the wall, about to burst onto the European scene to banish all metaphysical insight and conceptually level the cosmos in one great sweep, Ficino was drawing out from the Church's most orthodox sources an account of creation as both celestial music and sacred icon of the Godhead. Perhaps Ficino was able to see the need for this because, besides being a Christian humanist and a holy priest, Ficino was a Hermetic magician.

The Hermeticist and Catholic convert Valentin Tomberg explicitly framed the role of Hermeticism in the modern age as the rejection of rationalism, and the privileging of the concrete over all reductionist, isolated concepts detached from reality. In *Meditations on the Tarot*, which was published posthumously and anonymously in 1980, Tomberg wrote:

> The Hermetic-philosophical sense (or initiate sense) is that of concrete spiritual realities. The Hermeticist explains facts not by laws obtained

---

[3] Cornelio Fabro, "The Intensive Hermeneutics of Thomistic Philosophy: The Notion of Participation," *Review of Metaphysics* 27.3 (1974): 449–91, at 480.

by abstraction nor, much less still, by principles obtained by active abstraction, but rather by proceeding from abstract facts to more concrete beings in order to arrive at that which is the most concrete, that alone in existence which is absolutely concrete, i.e., God. Because for the initiate sense God is that which is most real, and therefore most concrete. In fact, amongst all that exists, God is that alone which is absolutely real and concrete, whilst created beings are only relatively real and concrete; and what we designate as "concrete fact" is in reality only an abstraction from divine reality.[4]

This, in a nutshell, is the "deeper worldview" of Christian Hermeticism. This is the vision that allows one to see spiritual realities not as speculative concepts that may or may not have some causal relation to one's life, but really *see* them as concrete realities. Having made its own the ontology that accommodates the revelation of God, the Hermetic mind, according to Tomberg, moves from the doctrines known as stated propositions to an existential encounter with the realities those doctrines convey, ultimately to the encounter with God Himself, present everywhere. All, then, is seen in the light of God's existence as the absolute *reality* on which everything rests, and everything is seen as relative to that secure and unchanging *reality*.

The Enlightenment, by its fragmentation of the mind into adversative parts that were once in harmony with one another under the old realism of the Western intelligence, bled out meaning from the world and thus made any encounter with God—of whom the world had hitherto been understood as a created communication—considerably difficult, if not impossible. Enlightenment Rationalism reduced reason to the possession of abstract principles that were judged to be more real than the chaotic concrete realities from which such principles became

---

[4] *Meditations on the Tarot: A Journey into Christian Hermeticism* (Brooklyn, NY: Angelico Press, n.d. [2020]), 95.

progressively unanchored. Of course, such a truncated conception of reason couldn't account for a vast range of human experience. In turn, Enlightenment Romanticism sprung up in an attempt to rescue what had been cut by rationalism from the human horizon. But having accepted the premises of rationalism—namely, that *reality* "out there" is reducible to the mere measurable and quantifiable—the Romantics located the realm of meaning, belonging, affectivity, and intimacy in enclosed impulses of the mind rather than seeing them as responses to the way the world *actually is*. Hence, the Romantic movement was typically accompanied by a solipsistic melancholy that stood in contrast to the naïve optimism of rationalism's confidence. By the time this process of dismantling the once integrated Western mind was complete, it was held that if "God" existed, he was probably a neurochemical in the prefrontal cortex.

If the faithful are to uncover a path out of the dual crisis of authority and meaning to which I referred above, which are themselves downstream from the initial Enlightenment spell, the faithful will have to double down on the devotional life. That will require a full recovery of the theocentrism that is antithetical to the "Enlightened," abstractionist, materialist paradigm of modernity. This cultivation of, as it were, a premodern conception of the world, is one I've pursued for years. When I wander with my dog in the fields or woods, or along the canals near my home in rural England, I behold the disclosing of the Godhead *in time*: the ongoing creative will of the Father, rendered intelligible through the Eternal Logos, animated and renewed by the Spirit. I'm not embarrassed to say that I'm often stirred to fall onto my knees and praise Him (behaviour that nearby farmers find alarming).

The urgent necessity before us is that of re-enchanting the material cosmos in which we find ourselves (as the topmost part), and doing so not by superimposing *meaning* onto it as if it were otherwise nothing but purposeless blobs in a vacuum. We must break the spell of the Enlightened man—who can only superficially be a Christian—and recover the vision of the cosmos as God's Icon by which God conveys Himself here and now. In short, I suggest, the venture of slowly salvaging our crumbling civilisation will start with the death of the Enlightened man and the rebirth of the Hermetic man. Indeed, the Hermetic vision may be exactly what's needed to break out of the modern paradigm. And if that's correct, then no sooner should the Hermetic vision be attained than it must be united to the Gospel proclamation and the sacramental power of the Church, otherwise it will rapidly degenerate into something indistinguishable from New Ageism, further plunging the West into the frustration of mere natural religion. Consider the following passage by the theologian and writer Stratford Caldecott:

> The New Age can...be understood as a reaction, or set of reactions, to the atomic individualism of post-Enlightenment modernity, and to the social fragmentation and alienation associated with this. In its negative aspect, it presents a picture of the self desperately battering against the bars of its own cage, trying to find a way out, but constrained by one or other unexamined assumption of modernity. It seeks to submit to an authority, but will no longer look in the one place where genuine authority is to be found. It seeks love, but it cannot bring itself to make a commitment. It seeks to respect and venerate nature, but at the same time it wants to escape the constraints of nature. It wants to become immortal, but at the same time to evolve into something different from itself. It wants to know everything, but not by becoming humble enough to learn. It wants to be free, but not by having to make a decision.[5]

Every one of these aspirations of New Ageism marks a wholesome rejection of, as Caldecott puts it, "the atomic

---

[5] Stratford Caldecott, *Understanding the New Age Movement* (London: The Catholic Truth Society, 2006), 36.

individualism of post-Enlightenment modernity." Each of
these aspirations represents a deep and sincere pursuit
of the truth, accompanied by an error that finds its
corrective only in the Christian life. Were the Church
to resume its mission of preaching the Gospel, cutting
through the coldness of the Enlightened heart of modern
man, freeing him, and inducting him into the mystical
life that is the Church's gift, that ancient institution
may begin to claw back some of its lost authority, too.

At present, what we're witnessing in the secular West is
the frustration of natural religion, unfulfilled by supernatural religion, haemorrhaging within the physicalist paradigm of modernity. The spirit of modern Western man
is like a faulty pressure cooker that's going to explode,
and every attempt to fix the problem pushes him further
into the false and malignant solutions of individualism,
statism, transhumanism, and all the deceitful promises
of the technological age that drive an ever-greater wedge
between our condition and any reconciliation with God's
creation—and ultimately any meeting with Him.

Only by recovering a love for its own tradition as a
gift providentially bestowed down the centuries will the
Church respond to the dual crisis of loss of meaning
and loss of authority. As I say, it is possible that, to
break the spell, the Church will have to turn once again
to the Hermetic vision: "Hermeticism," Tomberg tells us,

> insofar as it is a living tradition—for more than
> thirty centuries—owes its life to the command-
> ment "Honour thy father and thy mother"... Her-
> meticism lives and survives from century to cen-
> tury thanks to its essential faithfulness to the
> divine commandments "Thou shalt not kill" and
> "Honour thy father and thy mother."

The Church is thwarted in bestowing its gift upon
mankind because, in its ongoing repudiation of its own
tradition, it is currently preoccupied in killing its father
and mother.

Eastern Orthodox Christians—who still largely fulfil the fourth commandment by loving tradition—are, in this regard, at a certain advantage. Latin Christians have long emphasised "assent," and hence the possession of *ideas*, over existential transformation through right worship (an emphasis that has only swelled due to the unexamined acceptance of the rationalist paradigm). It is unsurprising, then, that serious Catholicism is more likely to be found online—where ideas are offered and bought up—than in the local church. And those Catholics who have retained the organic conception of the Church as the institution that gifts to the baptised the virtues of right relationality with God—a conception of the Christian as a *liturgical creature*—have for some time now been actively persecuted by the incumbents of the Church's highest offices. Such Catholics are seen as betrayers of the modern project of Enlightened man, whom the Church's leaders have enthroned in their demotion of Christ the King. And in seeing such Catholics in this way, the Church's government is entirely correct.

This enthronement of Enlightened man has sucked life out of the Church-polity, and thus the community of the baptised has become jaded and weary. With this, the role of the Blessed Virgin, which is to offer human nature to the Eternal Logos for supernatural transformation, has become eclipsed. As Tomberg puts it:

> The Virgin is not only the source of creative élan, but also of spiritual longevity. This is why the West, in turning away more and more from the Virgin, *is growing old*, i.e., it is distancing itself from the rejuvenating source of longevity. Each revolution which has taken place in the West—that of the Reformation, the French revolution, the scientific revolution, the delirium of nationalism, the communist revolution—has advanced the process of aging in the West, because each signified a further distancing from the principle of the Virgin.[6]

---

[6] Tomberg, *Meditations*, 294.

The Blessed Virgin brings spiritual regeneration to nature by welcoming the Logos into the inner chamber. Inasmuch as the Virgin is permitted to take up her role of co-creative mediatrix, the West, which is her child, may unite a sacral humanity with the Eternal Logos in a single, integrated, *personal* civilisation—as she once did with her *Fiat* to the Archangel. The cycle of revolution and repudiation, from which the West will never escape under Enlightened man, is rapidly aging the West, and it will continue to do so until the West obeys the fourth commandment and reinducts itself into its tradition. This revolutionary cycle has now fully entered the inner life of the Church, for which reason the only hope of the West, namely the Church's apostolic mission, has retreated into the shadows.

But what is this phenomenon called the West? It is the transfiguration by sanctifying grace of Hellenic wisdom, Roman imperialism and law, and the tradition of nations. Inasmuch as Christendom ever existed, it was merely the exoteric manifestation of this esoteric transformation. The principality of Satan and the City of Flesh are found in no particular place beyond the heart of man, and inasmuch as the world resembles the diabolic realm, it is merely reflecting the condition of man's heart. Likewise, the Kingdom of God and the City of God can be found nowhere but in the heart of man. In which dominion we live depends upon interior conversion: it depends upon which paradigm we opt for. When the Hermetic Joseph de Maistre called Enlightened man "satanical," this was not mere rhetoric or even metaphor; he was speaking at the deepest, most literal and univocal level.[7]

"Behold, the Kingdom of God is within you," says the Lord (Luke 17:21). It is necessary that the spell of

---

[7] Joseph de Maistre, *The Pope: Considered in His Relations with the Church, Temporal Sovereignties, Separated Churches, and the Cause of Civilization,* trans. Aeneas McDonell Dawson (London: C. Dolman, 1850), xxiii.

modernity be broken so that the scales may fall and this Kingdom be seen with the eyes of the spirit. This, I suggest, may be the new role of Hermeticism: to overcome the black magic of modernity with the sacred magic of the *prisca theologia*, that the unchaining of the Church may begin and its supernatural gifts be delivered once more.

5

THE MAGI RETURN

THE West is clearly entrenched in a "meaning crisis," whilst the institutional Church is in an "authority crisis" which has altogether moved it into what I've called its "post-authority epoch." Consequently, the only institution that I believe can adequately respond to the meaning crisis is in no condition to do so. I have suggested that this double crisis also represents two sides of the same problem: the slow bewitchment of the Western mind by the spell of the Enlightenment.

Having lost a sense of the supernatural, and having theologically justified this loss by decades of conflating the natural and the supernatural, the Church has lost a sense of its very purpose. What is now left is power, and a craving for power within a petty and dying bureaucracy. The Church's government has long run on the fumes of its previously held authority, but the engine is now choking and the whole institution is rapidly grinding to a halt. In a feeble attempt to hold onto the last vestiges of authority, the Church's government has resorted to the habitual exercise of arbitrary power, which, ironically, is further accelerating the erosion of clerical authority.

The Church must, it seems to me, recover its true *personality*—for a corporate Person she is—as the gift of God to all nations for the transformation of the human heart from stone to flesh (Ezekiel 36:26). The precondition for such a recovery, I have proposed, is that of breaking the spell of modernity, that the scales may fall from our eyes and we can again behold the participatory, vertical vision of creation as the emanated communication of the Godhead. The Hermetic tradition

may provide us with the ancient vernacular to understand this communication, so that we might receive—in
imitation of the Virgin—the divine Logos within, to
undergo the interior transfiguration for expelling the
darkness that has clouded the West.

We are in a post-Christian condition, and whilst post-
Christian man is not the same animal as pre-Christian
man, it is nonetheless true that we have entered a new
form of paganism, with the dual characteristics of paganism prevailing as the dominant facets of our shared life:
idolatry and *slavery to appetite*. These two characteristics
always go together. We exist for a shared purpose, and
once that shared purpose becomes eclipsed, we incrementally shut ourselves up to pursue individual private ends,
which become increasingly associated with the personal
gratification of appetite. Thus, the religious impulse that
directs us to the attainment of our shared purpose gets
transferred onto commodities and sensual satisfactions,
and these become the idols of post-religious religiosity,
which ultimately serve the idol of the isolated self—that
final post-religious illusion. What's unique about the
"progressive-liberal" settlement that is the proper polity
of the new paganism is that it celebrates this process
of enslavement by commodification and titillation as
the highest civilisational achievement.

Just as astrologers and magicians of old were directed
to the Incarnate Word in the cave to offer Him all in
man's nature that required supernatural transformation—
man's religious impulse (represented by frankincense),
his temporal needs (represented by gold), and his death
which was to become new life (represented by myrrh)—
so too post-Christian man must approach the cave of
the Church, that he may wander in the desert no more.
Where the Truth presently remains veiled and obscured
by the black magic of the Enlightenment, the Hermetic
path possibly presents us with a way for modern man
to approach this hallowed cave. And this Hermetic path

turns out to be a very ancient path indeed, much treasured by the Church at various times down the ages.

Whether Hermeticism and Neoplatonism have the exact same genealogy is a question for historians. In any case, they have ever been inextricably bound together. Neoplatonism provides the ontological superstructure within which a theocentric worldview makes sense, and Hermeticism provides practices and disciplines for acquiring the habit of this theocentric vision. This superstructure is that on which the Church Fathers, the medieval schoolmen, and the Christian humanists of the Renaissance built their civilisational project. Many great thinkers of those epochs posited notions that have since become bizarre to us because we've lost the framework within which they lived.

Typically, Christians are uneasy at any mention of Hermeticism or esotericism. This is understandable, for such terms have come to mean anything that is not modern mainstream Christian spirituality. In this way, "Hermeticism" is rather like the term "alternative medicine," which doesn't tell you what it is but what it's not, namely not modern mainstream medicine. Thus, "alternative medicine" can mean anything from eating cooked elderberries to support one's immune system, to Reiki. Likewise, depending on what one is reading, "Hermetic" or "esoteric" could mean anything from the Tombergian practice of "concentration without effort" (a practice similar to those recommended in Jean Pierre de Caussade's *Abandonment to Divine Providence*) to the demonic sex magic of Aleister Crowley.

What I mean by "Hermetic" is a set of practices and disciplines of mind, will, and imagination that habituate the practitioner to a vision of the world that acknowledges it as God's Icon. This, I claim, was the shared vision of premodernity, and more generally the shared metaphysical vernacular of all broadly religious ontologies. And it is the vision we have to recover if we're to break the spell that established modern man, who is a disintegrated, centaurial creature due to his acceptance of the rationalist paradigm and his retreat from grace.

To indicate how disenchanted our world has become, one can imagine the reaction of his coreligionists to a Catholic saying, "Because I take the Christian conception of the world seriously, I've decided to become a crystal healer." *But that's New Ageism!* would be the expected reply. And yet, the Common Doctor of the Church, Thomas Aquinas, argues that the presence of precious metals can prevent depression and sapphires can stop bleeding. (He also held that humans possess innate psychic powers—powers he believed would always lead to evil if not united to the actions of saints, angels, or Divine Persons: see ST I, Q. 117, art. 3, ad 2.) Hildegard von Bingen dedicated Book Four of her *Physica* to the use of crystals, gems, and stones to heal a myriad of ailments, and she included guidance on how to "recharge" one's healing stones in the morning sun or the glow of a full moon. Now, I'm not saying that St. Thomas and St. Hildegard were necessarily correct in these views, but the fact that these teachings are so far beyond what's acceptable among modern Catholics indicates how far from Christianity's premodern worldview we have strayed. This is especially interesting in the case of St. Hildegard, given that she declared that no part of her teaching on healing was learned by experience (though she claimed it was confirmed by experience), but received by direct private revelation from God—a claim that was known when she was made a Doctor of the Church in 2012. These are not peripheral authorities in the Church.

Others want to claim that Hermeticism is a species of Gnosticism. *Gnosis* for the Hermeticist, however, means something very different from the "gnosis" of the Gnostics.[1] Whereas the Gnostics believed in hidden knowledge that was undisclosed to those who weren't spiritually pure

---

[1] See Jean Borella, *The Truth of Christian Gnosis*, trans. G. John Champoux (Brooklyn, NY: Angelico Press, 2023).

or enlightened enough, the *gnosis* of the Hermeticist is not hidden knowledge but *deeper* knowledge of that which is known to all who are free from the spells—the "egregores," to use a Hermetic phrase—of materialism, rationalism, and other such ancient superstitions that have reemerged to create modernity. That the Hermeticist pursues deeper knowledge of what's known, rather than secret knowledge of what's hidden, is explicitly declared and defended at the beginning of Tomberg's *Meditations*.[2] Moreover, Gnosticism has invariably led to a disdain for the material world and thus a contempt for the body, supported by an anthropological dualism which divided man into a spiritual substance in a fleshly cage. Hermeticism, however, seeks the opposite, namely the retrieval of the world as divine communication and the reintegration of the human person as a single substance of embodied spirit.[3]

When St. Albert the Great, Doctor of the Church, translated a principal Hermetic text called the *Emerald Tablet* into Latin for his students at the University of Paris, he did so because he believed they had something to learn from it.[4] The first principle of the *Tablet* establishes the precondition for the Hermetic vision, namely the vertical, participatory, Neoplatonic conception of creation:

> True it is, without falsehood, certain and most true. That which is above is like to that which is below, and that which is below is like to that which is above, to accomplish the miracles of one thing. And as all things were by contemplation of one, so all things arose from this one thing by a single act of adaptation.

According to the *Tablet*, the realm we inhabit is a reflection of that which is transcendent, and this acknowledgement has always been understood by Hermeticists as the prerequisite for "sacred magic" ("to accomplish

---

[2] See Tomberg, *Meditations*, 5–7.
[3] Or, better yet, intellectualised body, as Fr Aidan Nichols once put it (with greater Thomistic precision).
[4] See Tomberg, 21–23.

miracles," as the *Tablet* puts it), which is their term for
that species of blessing that heals by mediation what is
spiritually corrupted. Creation, the *Tablet* tells us, unfolds
out of God's contemplation of His own Mystery, and
we fulfil the "adaptation" of that creation by rationally
and lovingly participating in the eternal act of divine
contemplation—known to Christians as the communion
of love in the Triune Godhead. The *Tablet* was translated
by St. Albert, it seems, because he wanted his students
to deepen their knowledge of things known.

In his remarkable essay entitled "Hermetic Imagination,"[5] Charles Coulombe presents some of Hermeticism's
pedigree in the Church Universal:

> The meeting of Hermeticism (the belief that the
> visible world is an analogy of the invisible, summed
> up in the phrase "as above, so below") and Neo-
> platonism (with its insistence that the Platonic
> Archetypes were the realities, of which earthly
> expressions were mere shadows) with Christian-
> ity produced several waves of educated folk who
> shared this magical concept of the world. First
> came such Neoplatonic Church Fathers as St. Dio-
> nysius the Areopagite, St. Clement of Alexandria,
> Origen, and St. Augustine. Then came the Ultra-
> Realist scholastics such as John Scotus Eriugena,
> Pope Sylvester II, William of Auvergne, Roger Bacon,
> Bl. Raymond Lully, St. Bonaventure, and St. Alber-
> tus Magnus, many of whom looked to Alchemy,
> Astrology, and the Qabalah as a means of interpret-
> ing the revelation implicit in creation—a revelation
> supplementary, but inferior, to Holy Writ. Lastly,
> the Classical Humanists such as Reuchlin, Pico
> della Mirandola, Cardinal Bessarion and Aeneas
> Piccolomini were similarly inclined. The Refor-
> mation put an end to most such developments.

Among the list of names that Coulombe provides, Fathers,
Doctors, Saints, and Blesseds are counted as having
adopted the Hermetic path. And as he notes, the age of

---

[5] Charles A. Coulombe, "Hermetic Imagination: The Effect of The Golden
Dawn on Fantasy Literature," https://dc.swosu.edu/mythlore/vol21/iss2/52/.

revolution, which the Reformation inaugurated, began the process of eclipsing the world understood as God's Icon—a process which would eventually give us modern man, who stumbles in the dark whilst calling himself "enlightened." In the same essay we learn that the Baron de Sarachaga, a relation of St. Teresa of Avila, for forty years headed the Hermetic Institut des Fastes, approved by Popes Pius IX and Leo XIII. "Pierre Dujois, a learned Hermeticist," Coulombe tells us, "wrote of this school in 1912: 'There exists in Paray-le-Monial [the centre of devotion to the Sacred Heart of Jesus] a mysterious Cabalic centre, sincerely Catholic it seems, and where the bizarre orthodoxy is nevertheless accepted and even encouraged by the Church.'"

Why has Hermetic Neoplatonism enjoyed such a rich pedigree in the Church? The answer may be in the fact that it possesses the double advantage of overcoming the problem of "ascent" in classical Platonism, by presenting a conception of the world as disclosing by emanation the Eternal Mystery *here* and *now* in the concrete complexus of experience, *and* of providing mystical practices by which to spiritually unite oneself—or better, allow oneself to be united—with this Mystery. Classical Platonic ascent holds that the reality is not to be found in this world, which is deemed a deceptive shadow of the perennial "forms" that constitute *true* reality. According to this view, this non-empirical but nevertheless intelligible realm can be accessed only by those who, using reason alone, undertake the intellectual journey required to ascend towards it.

This is an account of truth that simply cannot accommodate the biblical view of history, which sees the truth unfolding in the temporal events of peoples and nations, nor can it accommodate the central Mystery of the Incarnation, which is God's direct spoken Word embodied in the Nazarene—a person living at a particular time in a particular place. But Hermetic Neoplatonism construes "ascent" as acknowledgement of—and spiritual harmony with—the temporal world as the communication of the Godhead. And whilst creation is not the reality in an absolute sense, which is God alone, creation truly conveys Him as my speech truly conveys me. That the world is fallen and wounded by sin doesn't undermine the Neoplatonic view of creation as divine communication, but only accentuates the need for the healing and elevating power of grace for creation's fulfilment.

In fact, it is very likely that what the Church in large part needs is something like the Franciscan movement of the thirteenth century. Franciscanism was, in essence, a grassroots recovery of the Patristic Neoplatonism that saw creation as God's Icon, which linked this enchanted vision to a practical call to embody the mystery of the Incarnation in the most radical, lived expression of the Gospel. St. Francis and his followers soon had many lay folk, entire families even, joining them, eventually forming the Third Order. Franciscanism transformed medieval Christendom, and yet the movement looked very similar to many heretical sects of the time. Had you seen an early Franciscan, you might have struggled to tell him apart from a Waldensian, a Bogomil, or an Albigensian. They lived in a very similar manner to these heretical groups, and shared similar aspirations. The Franciscans were distinguished, however, by their unswerving loyalty to Christian orthodoxy and the institutional structures of the Church. This, though, was a loyalty that they maintained while simultaneously enlarging the parameters of what was then deemed orthodoxy.

We are today dealing with a proliferation of heretical movements, and it may be that our response will involve expanding the parameters of orthodoxy whilst remaining steadfastly loyal to the ancient Faith and the Church— despite its current condition. Stratford Caldecott, in his booklet on the New Age, writes that modern man has been fundamentally detraditioned. Indeed, we may be the first people like this: a people inducted into no tradition except a tradition of repudiation of tradition. Inasmuch as we are religious, we stand in judgement over religious tradition, selecting from it what we please in a spirit of postmodern self-authorship. This ultimately leads to nihilism for the single reason that *meaning* is always something before which one must humble oneself, and over which one cannot stand in judgement without it vanishing. Caldecott doesn't hesitate to highlight the Hermetic writings of Valentin Tomberg as offering a path through this novel territory:

> The Christian community can expect a generation of converts to come from outside the tradition, from a radically post-modern, new age, and neo-pagan milieu. An influential example would be the Russian anthroposophist Valentin Tomberg, who died in 1973 after converting to Catholicism and writing anonymously a massive work entitled *Meditations on the Tarot* intended to reintegrate the lost wisdom of the Hermetic tradition with the orthodox Christianity of St. Teresa, St. Francis, and St. Bonaventure... Despite its considerable flaws, it can stand as a harbinger, perhaps, of other attempts to retrieve and purify the legacy of the esoteric movements.[6]

Note that Caldecott does not say that Tomberg sought to integrate, but *reintegrate*, the Hermetic tradition with orthodox Christianity; the implication being that Hermeticism as a spiritual path once had its home in the Church but has been sundered from her. Caldecott suggests that, notwithstanding its faults, Tomberg's *Meditations* may be at the genesis of a wider project—a necessary project—of retrieving and purifying in the light of the Gospel the practices and disciplines of Hermeticism.

Countless Christians have been inspired by Tomberg's writings. Pope John Paul II was photographed with both volumes of the *Meditations* on his desk. The philosopher

---

[6] Caldecott, *Understanding the New Age Movement*, 54.

and defender of Catholic traditionalism Robert Spaemann wrote a foreword to the work, a fact which in my view stands very much in its favour. Cardinal Hans Urs von Balthasar wrote an afterword, which stands less in its favour. Many have come into the Church from without by way of Tomberg's writings. An important case is that of Roger Buck. Buck was once a committed member of the neo-pagan Findhorn Community and later a leading New Age activist in England, during which time he had important contact with many of the most renowned leaders in both the British and American New Age Movements. But his ongoing study of Tomberg's Hermeticism gradually led him to the Church. He's now a respected Catholic author, having written such remarkable works as *The Gentle Traditionalist* (two companion volumes) and *Cor Jesu Sacratissimum: From Secularism and the New Age to Christendom Renewed.*[7] As Buck has written, "It was only through my repeated reading of Tomberg's deconstruction of paganism that I could free myself from the New Age."

Tomberg deconstructs paganism precisely because he is engaged in recovering the nature-supernature distinction that is the cornerstone of Christianity, which many twentieth-century theologisers strove to undermine. If the dual imperative before us, for the Church to breathe once more, is that of recovering the cosmos as a theophanic mystery and recovering the nature-supernature distinction, as I've proposed throughout this chapter and the preceding chapters, then Tomberg is our ally. The hope is that, as the wisdom of the Hermetic way is unveiled, so too will the spell of modernity be broken, and the following realisation about which Tomberg writes so beautifully will be undergone by many more people:

---

[7] Roger Buck, *The Gentle Traditionalist: A Catholic Fairy-Tale from Ireland* (Kettering, OH: Angelico Press, 2015); *Cor Jesu Sacratissimum: From Secularism and the New Age to Christendom Renewed* (Kettering, OH: Angelico Press, 2017); *The Gentle Traditionalist Returns: A Catholic Knight's Tale from Ireland* (Brooklyn, NY: Angelico Press, 2019).

The way of Hermeticism, solitary and intimate as
it is, comprises authentic experiences from which
it follows that the Roman Catholic Church is,
in fact, a depository of Christian spiritual truth,
and the more one advances on the way of free
research for this truth, the more one approaches
the Church. Sooner or later one inevitably experiences that spiritual reality corresponds—with
an astonishing exactitude—to what the Church
teaches: that there are guardian Angels; that there
are saints who participate actively in our lives;
that the Blessed Virgin *is* real...that the sacraments *are* effective, and that there are seven of
them—and not two, or three, or even eight; that
the three sacred vows—of obedience, chastity, and
poverty—constitute in fact the very essence of all
authentic spirituality; that prayer is a powerful
means of charity, for beyond as well as here below;
that the ecclesiastical hierarchy reflects the celestial hierarchical order; that the Holy See and the
papacy represent a mystery of divine magic; that
hell, purgatory, and heaven *are* realities; that, lastly,
the Master himself—although he loves everyone,
Christians of all confession as well as all non-
Christians—abides with his Church, since he is
always present there, since he visits the faithful
there and instructs his disciples there.[8]

So, *can Hermetic magic rescue the Church?* I must con-
clude with a qualified *no*. Obviously, Hermeticism cannot
rescue the Church. The Church has a Saviour, and that
is the Lord Jesus Christ. He alone can rescue the Church,
and so He will, for the Church must continue until the
conclusion of the world. Christ walks this earth today,
however, in His members. The baptised are other christs,
and they are called evermore to become such by sacramental—principally, Eucharistic—transformation. Whilst
they remain under the spell of Enlightened man, that
warlock who has conjured modernity, and before whom
the Church's hierarchy presently quakes, the Church's

---

[8] Tomberg, *Meditations*, 281–82.

members will continue to stagger and their mission will increasingly ebb. Tomberg claimed that the time had come for the Church to engage once more with the Hermetic way, to discern what could be embraced within the broad sphere of Christian spirituality and what could *not* be accommodated. Such an engagement may now be a pressing necessity.

Again, I declare that Christ alone can rescue His Church, but we have ousted Him in a diabolic effort to divorce Bride from Bridegroom. We have lost the primacy of the supernatural: however much the Lord may seek to rescue His Church from its current trajectory of self-destruction, He finds a Church whose members largely don't believe they need rescuing. They are under a spell, and that spell must be broken. Perhaps the sacred magic of Hermes Trismegistus is what's needed to banish the black magic of Enlightened man. And thereby, we may begin to retrieve *meaning*, and in turn start the Church's process of humbling itself before the true King of the Universe.

When one enters the Cathedral of Siena, the first thing one sees is a huge fifteenth-century floor mosaic of Hermes Trismegistus (Plate 2) welcoming visitors onto the path of theocentric wonder, by which they may learn the wisdom to humble themselves before the One who resides in the sanctuary at the other end of the building. Perhaps having so humbled itself, the Church's government may recover some of its lost authority. There is no chance of that, though, until the hierarchy is freed from the bewitchment of modernity, to take up its mission once more of sanctifying the faithful and making disciples of all nations, rather than yielding to the unbaptised world—which is the principality of Satan, and that mission's incessant enemy.

PLATE 2
Anonymous, *Hermes Trismegistus* (c. 1488)
Floor mosaic in the Cathedral of Siena

6

THE MAGIC OF CHRISTMAS IS REAL

DURING Advent, when the Church prepares herself for Christmas, her members enter a time of mortification and penance as they await the coming of the child Jesus. Frequent invitations to drink mulled wine and eat mince pies with brandy butter in the weeks preceding Christmas Day can make this difficult. One way to observe Advent, however, is to eat less meat. Fortunately, during that very time of the year, easily hunted mushrooms—beings that belong to a kingdom between the animal and plant kingdoms—appear across much of the countryside. One Advent season, I strolled into a well-manured grassland to discover hundreds of field blewits. There they were before me, great jellyish saucers standing on purple stems in terrific fairy rings across the green pasture.

Fairies had obviously been gathering at night for their hibernal celebrations. They likely danced and laughed, played tricks on one another, and fell about amid the ribaldry that is the inevitable effect of those pixie draughts from fermented hawthorn berries. The evidence of this was all around me. Those mushrooms marked the sacred circles of the sprites with whom we share our landscape, whose rights and entitlements we disregard.

Due to the mental fog of late modernity that incrementally distorted our vision, we grew blind to the iconographic character of the world around us, and so the fairies disappeared. Slowly, we ceased to see that things are not only substances but symbols. Modern people would never call a fungal formation of spore-scattering fruits from a complex underground mycelial web a "fairy ring," just as modern people, when carving a pathway for horseless carriages through the rustic countryside that our ancestors gifted us, do not call it "Hollybush Road" or "Brown Cow Lane" or "The Great Eastern Way" or some other such name, but the "M650" or the "A14." Everything in late modernity is *instrumental* rather than meaningful, formulaic rather than poetic, and consequently grey rather than colourful. We reduced all insight, inspiration, understanding, comprehension, contemplation, appreciation, observation, discernment, and awareness to the one quantitative category of "information," and thereby emptied our minds of all that really matters—and the world we have made around us reflects this cognitive corruption.

Many Christian philosophers and theologians have attempted to rectify this situation by arguing in defence of *telos*. They say that if you can see that substances, at least living ones, develop and act for an end—that is, they have a *telos*—then from this principle you can retrieve meaning and purpose. Certain Humean and analytic philosophers with truncated imaginations—and hence truncated minds—have called such teleological arguments "magical thinking." But in fact, such arguments are not magical at all, and that is precisely their problem. In my view, attempting to retrieve meaning and purpose in late modernity by appealing to teleology is problematic not because it is magical, but because it is not magical *enough*.

I can state the *end* for which mushrooms exist, namely to spread spores for the perpetuation of the mycelium of which they are upward hanging fruits—but no part of that account requires the existence of fairies. When our ancestors saw mushrooms in a circle in a field, they didn't just see what those mushrooms were *for*, they saw symbols. The reason for this, I suggest, is because they understood that knowing the *end* for which mushrooms appear is insufficient to know why God wanted a universe in which mushrooms exist at all. For *that*, you need a symbolic or "iconographic" account of the cosmos, by which you can see creation as *divine language*—that is, as an expression of the Eternal Word.

For premoderns, the cosmos wasn't merely composed of substances that each acted for some end; those substances in different ways were *words* of God, as He conveyed His inner life. In the premodern view, deciphering the iconography of creation was essential to understanding the world as participating in, and emanating from, the Divine Mind.

To give one example, it is not obvious what the *telos* of a rainbow is. (Try to forget for a moment the unfortunate connotations of rainbows in our own age.) A rainbow, of course, isn't a substance at all. It is an effect of refracted light entering the eye, which is itself an effect of multiple conditions of various substances coming together. One can indicate what a philosopher might call the "efficient causes" at play for the rainbow to come about as an effect. But the man of premodern intellectual habits wants to ask: what did God want to convey by creating a world in which rainbows were possible at all?

The biblical answer to the above question is: His own benignity. It is fortunate that a biblical answer is available, but otherwise such answers are open neither to the scientist nor to the philosopher. To the seeker of mystical *gnosis*, the seeker of the inner meaning of the world as a divine language and a realm of iconographic meaning, such answers are the most important answers. If he can understand that "language"—the very language spoken on Mount Horeb and heard by the Prophet Elijah—then he can learn to speak it in the silent idiom of his heart in harmony with Him whose language it is.

At Christmas, children the world over receive gifts from a flying saint dressed in a bright red outfit, who is pulled across the earth a hundred feet above its surface by a small herd of reindeer. This yuletide god of the north was likely first seen by the ancestors of the Sami. The peoples of Lapland used to feed red mushrooms with white spots—that is, the fly agaric mushroom—to their reindeer and then drink the urine. All the psychoactive properties of those toadstools were still in the urine without any of the dangerous toxicity, which had been neutralised by the reindeers' kidneys. After those rounds of cervine excretion, the Laplanders saw reindeer flying around them, dragging a man dressed as a fly agaric mushroom. And these visions disclosed to them something of the world's inner meaning. They peered into a realm where divinised spirits constantly interact with the natural world, transforming it, guiding the lives of lesser beings, and causing creation to glorify its Creator in a chorus of incalculable voices.

That same world, however, is also racked and frustrated by sin, darkness, and suffering, and this truth presents to the theocentric mind the most menacing challenge to its vision. And yet it is to this point that the Christmas story is the greatest possible answer. The whole universe, down to the tiniest particle, is afflicted by sin. Sin is creation's failure to glorify the Creator, its failure to speak the divine language—a failure, according to the Christian account, that *we* wove into the cosmos with the fabric of our pride.

In the Christmas story, God, beholding His creation's endarkening, commissioned one of the innumerable angelic spirits that are operating everywhere and at all times. And God sent that living force to a part of His creation that He, in a fit of heavenly insanity, had plucked up from the mire of the earth. At the very moment of its inception, He had elevated that speck of the universe above all hate and envy and guile, and thus above all death. That is, God chose an imperceptible fragment of His creation, which was also creation's perfection, and, from all eternity, He called it by the name of Mary—thereafter, all generations would call her blessed. From that maiden, hidden in obscurity, the inner language of the Godhead, the Eternal Word itself, from which all existence derives its intelligibility, drew the whole cosmos back into itself in a moment of embodiment both celestial and terrestrial.

The whole cosmos was concentrated and completed in one young lady, and from her the Eternal Word—Itself pouring forth from the amorous communion of the Godhead—drew created nature. By so doing, the Incarnation burst into creation like a lightning bolt flashing across a midnight landscape. No artist has captured this better than Tintoretto with his *Annunciation* of 1587 (Plate 3), in which, as the Archangel Gabriel appears before Mary, all the darkness, decay, and devastation of a world haunted by disobedience and self-destruction is flooded with divine love.

Nine months later, magicians, conjurers of the hidden language, who could read the symbolic universe, deciphered the grammar of the stars. And they meditated upon visitations experienced when wandering in the dreamworld. Those enigmatic men walked in piety across the dunes, obedient to the language of creation and the spirits that animate and recreate it at every moment. And at the end of their pilgrimage, they met the Centre of History as He lay there in a trough, whimpering and shivering amid stinking livestock, under the protection of the cosmic Magna Mater. Those royal magicians of the Eastern mysteries knew what they beheld because they understood the theophany of the universe, that cosmic icon that conveyed to them the Mystery that now struggled incarnate within their gaze. And they responded with symbols, which they lay before their vulnerable and helpless Creator.

Late modernity is a kind of hex on the human mind, and it has produced a people who can no longer read—let alone speak—the divine communication. When modernity

PLATE 3
Jacopo Tintoretto, *The Annunciation* (1583–1587)
Scuola Grande di San Rocco

split the world into the *res cogitans* and the *res extensa*—
the inner world of meaning and the external world of
atoms—in one sweep it silenced the divine language,
or rather it blocked up our senses. For us, the world
stopped speaking and became lifeless *stuff*.

First, the sacred places lost their sanctity, for the
only sacrality was deemed that of the inner man. The
grottos, the holy wells, and the sanctuaries became
neglected. A concrete warehouse was judged as good
a church as a Gothic masterpiece, for ultimately they
were both just heaps of atoms. What mattered, it was
thought, was holy feelings, not holy places. The whole
world was eventually emptied of its holiness, and one
day we looked up and surveyed the panorama and
all we could see was *stuff*. And all that stuff was grey.
"Never mind," we thought, and we turned inward to
take refuge in the holiness of the inner self, but to
our horror and ongoing despair we discovered that
nothing was there.

Our ancestors saw beyond that which is only disclosed to the body's eyes. The land was once covered in
glades and groves consecrated by the rituals of holy men
and women, and powerful spirits delighted in dwelling
in those places so pleasing to God. Those sacred hollows
are now under motorways and carparks, and everything
has become *stuff*. Now we think that fairy parties at
mushroom rings and flying reindeer carrying saints are
things out of which eventually we must grow up, when
in fact they belong to the realm inhabited only by those
who are mature enough to understand the world for
what it is: one great cathedral in which a billion cosmic
liturgies are celebrated. There, in the nave of creation,
the ultimate imperative is to join our voices to the
anthems of praise. That world is still there; we have only
to let the scales fall from our eyes. There is a black spell
on the human mind—that much is clear—but fear not:
it can be broken by the magic of Christmas.

7

INCARNATION AND EGREGORE

THE term "egregore" belongs to Hermetic philosophy and to Western esotericism more broadly. The notion of "egregore" is not dissimilar to that of "tulpa" in Tibetan Buddhism, the latter being a spiritual agent generated by the intense concentration of an elite monastic practitioner. "Egregore" is different, however, because according to the simplest definition, it is a spiritual force that arises out of the *collective commitment of a people to a falsehood.*

I once thought that I was eccentric in appealing to the notion of "egregores" to explain, at least in part, the chaotic world of ideological squabbles that we now inhabit. But then, some years ago, I attended a dinner at a friend's farmstead. During the meal, a discussion began concerning the future of the British Conservative Party. Everything indicated that the topic was going to be tiresome, when unexpectedly a youngish man at the other end of the table opined: "There is no hope for the Tories until they are somehow freed from the egregore that's been controlling them since the time of Robert Peel." I looked up from my venison cutlet in astonishment, an emotion that intensified as all those around the table nodded in agreement as if the young man had only commented upon the weather. Many there are, it seems, who in trying to explain our civilisational collapse are looking to the peripheries of the wider spiritual tradition of the West.

The exact metaphysical structure of egregores continues to be disputed. It remains obscure how human beings can, merely by thoughts and words, generate a spiritual being and then be bound and fettered by such a spirit. The reason for this ambiguity is partly because egregores only make sense when considered within a category of knowledge and practice too readily dismissed today, namely *magic*. The art of magic precisely holds that special words and incantations, with gestures and the use of distinct artefacts, accompanied by extreme mental concentration, can together possess a causal power beyond what belongs to common communication.

The Western world has always believed in magic. It has always held that curses exist and that they can be placed on people, animals, plants, fungi, and inanimate objects. And the Western world has always held that such curses can be banished by special words, special objects, and special concentration, which in that order it has been content to call "blessings," "sacramentals," and "prayer." In short, even the most orthodox in the West have always believed in what the Hermeticist calls the opposing forces of "goetia," or black magic, and "theurgy," or sacred magic—though they generally would not put it in such terms.

One may retort that when a person blesses a cursed object, God and His mediating saints and angels bring about the effect, not the person who is blessing. Perhaps, but neither is the person doing the blessing accidental to the process of banishing the curse. Conversely, black magic has its effects on account of the operation of demons, but that doesn't mean that the spellcasting warlock is accidental to the evil manifested—he clearly is a necessary part. Hence, we can think of egregores as generated curses that arise from the kind of concentration entailed by collective commitment to falsehoods. Egregores, then, are essentially hexes which take on lives of their own and, in turn, assume control of their conjurers.

The Christian mind is inclined to understand all evil spirits as demons. Demons, however, belonging as they do to the angelic genus, transcend human beings in the ontological *chain of being* employed by the Church's traditional theology. That is why demons descended—or "fell," to use the more homiletic terminology—from above to below. Egregores, on the other hand, rise from below to above, being conjured by human minds enslaved by error. In the words of Valentin Tomberg, an egregore "owes his existence to collective generation from below." But just as blessings are not angels, yet do require angels to bring about their effects, so too egregores are not demons, but they do emerge in part through the action of demons and are themselves at least demonic.

This may all sound rather antiquated and maybe quite bizarre, but we all still seem nonetheless to believe in magic, or at least act we as if magic were real. To observe a crowd of protestors marching through the streets, chanting some mindless slogan over and over with various gestures and performances, is to witness collective commitment to an *idea*, which the people in question believe will be realised through united incantations. Often, such people cannot explain what they want and how they think they will get it. They just *know*, in a way mysterious to everyone, including themselves, that they are righteous and that they are being led by something. As Joseph de Maistre detected, the people did not lead the Revolution; the Revolution led the people.[1] In such cases, it looks a lot like we are dealing with egregores.

Whilst believing it has outgrown such "delusions," the Western world continues to believe in both blessings and curses. It wasn't long ago that the Catholic Church's hierarchy got itself into hot water over this very matter when its curia issued the document *Fiducia Supplicans*, a formal declaration permitting priests to bless "irregular couples," including same-sex couples. (The document only permits blessings of the people in those irregular unions, not of the unions themselves; but given that any couple receiving such a blessing will present themselves

---

[1] Joseph de Maistre, *Considerations on France*, ed. Richard A. Lebrun (Cambridge: Cambridge University Press, 1994), 5.

as a union, the document's distinction is one without a difference, and thus a work of base sophistry.) Basically, the Church's leadership broke under pressure from those who have rejected the Christian religion's anthropology and moral framework, and more than that, they rejected the very notion that there is any opposition between the Church and the world—an opposition on which the very imperative to preach the Gospel is established.

Having rejected the life of nature, which the life of grace elevates and transforms, people in such unions nevertheless wanted to be blessed by the Church. The Church's leaders, as we should have anticipated, yielded. But the question remains: what *is* this strange, intangible thing called a "blessing" that is coveted by those who reject the worldview to which it belongs? And why is it so important that even deviants and secularists desire to receive one?

Maybe, one might suggest, the desire to receive a blessing stems from nothing more than a basic need for approval. But had the Church merely issued a memo declaring that it approved of—or at least did not con-demn—homosexual unions, that would have been widely deemed insufficient. The immediate response would have been to ask, "Then why can't we receive a blessing?" The fact is, as embarrassing as it might seem, we still believe that special words said with special concentra-tion, perhaps combined with special gestures and special artefacts, can possess a special causal power when aided by special, powerful spirits. That is, we still believe in magic, even the most secularised among us.

Many a time, I have had the experience of speaking with someone and suddenly realising that my interloc-utor is so captured by a set of ideological abstractions that he cannot conceive of an idea unless it is couched in the terms of his *a priori* commitments—during which process the idea will likely get lost in any case. The prob-lem is similar to that of disagreeing on a first principle, which, as Aristotle observed, makes further dialogue impossible. Ultimately, I find that my converser inhabits a different epistemic universe led by different forces. In short, I find him to be under an egregore.

Some time ago, I visited an old friend, a monk, at his priory. He and I discussed the notion of egregores in some depth. Eventually he said, "It seems to me that what the Hermetic tradition calls 'egregore,' the mainstream Christian tradition would call 'antichrist.'" Then, I thought: *what, indeed, could antichrist—the antithesis of Christ—be?* The spiritual Logos descended into matter, while egregores are spiritual error-structures that arise from the material plain. The truth became incarnate, while egregores are falsehoods that become spirits. The Incarnation is one; egregores are many.

Perhaps, then, when we read the following words of Saint John the Divine, it is the danger of egregores that we ought to have in mind: "Many antichrists have come; therefore, we know that it is the last hour. They went out from us, but they were not of us" (1 John 2:18–19). What are these "antichrists," these many beings that have their source in us but are not—or are no longer—part of us? I venture to suggest that the Beloved Disciple is warning the Church about the reign of egregores.

The "reign of egregores" is something to which we are now fully accustomed, whether we would use that phrase or not. In many respects, the twentieth century was the great epoch of the egregores. During World War II, the egregores of fascism, communism, and liberalism—all spawn of the great egregore of 1789—took control of entire populations and drove them into violence. True, the forces of evil lost the war, but from that, it does not follow that the forces of good won the war. The egregore of liberalism emerged triumphant, and almost no one who fought in that diabolical conflict, which saw the baptised murder the baptised, really knew what he was fighting for.

In the decades immediately following that colossal war of the egregores, the nations of the West embraced the rapid atomisation of the individual, the disunion of the sexes, the erosion of the family, the dissemination of pornography, the murder of the unborn, and the celebration of homosexuality, all aided and fomented with legislative acts. Ancient cities were transformed into colourless, concrete pens. Our musical tradition was discarded in favour of a thudding, torturous background noise. Our clothes were replaced with plastic coverings made by distant child slaves. And all the while, we were told that the name of what we beheld was "freedom."

The war's veterans were condemned to look on with bewilderment as the lands for which they'd fought were remade into an earthly hell. Even now, all the curses of the egregore of liberalism can hardly be questioned—even by self-identified "conservatives" (who quickly learn to celebrate them anyway)—without receiving a tirade of outrage from those under the spell of "progress."

As I have suggested, a truth that has become incarnate is the antithesis of a falsehood that has grown into a spirit. The Incarnation of the Eternal Logos in Jesus Christ is the great pivotal repudiation of the reign of egregores in history. For this reason, life in Christ—"the Way," as the early Christians called their religion—is the *only way* out. And the Incarnation is extended through innumerable creative and dynamic ways in our civilisation, a civilisation that is still running on the fumes of Christendom.

In the temporal sphere and at the level of the State, the most important among those creative and dynamic ways is *monarchy*. Indeed, it ought not to surprise us that World War II was largely presided over by elected autocrats—a war that never would have happened were it not for the egregore of secular nationalism, which had pitted monarch against monarch in World War I in a bid to eliminate the royal principle altogether.

Above all else, monarchy privileges the particular, the personal, and the incarnate. Monarchy teaches a people that they are not bound to pledge their allegiance to a symbol, a paper constitution, or an abstract ideological schema. They can pledge their allegiance to a family, and a member of that family who will—by sitting upon the throne, wearing the diadem, and being anointed by the hand of a bishop—embody the whole nation; and by so doing, he will pledge allegiance to *them*.[2]

The whole mystery of the corporate person of the nation—which is a true *person* who can be blamed, honoured, and even discipled (Matthew 28:19)—is distilled into the individual person of the monarch. For a sceptred nation, the *truth* of the national genius is concentrated in the monarch and revered as such. Hence, at the deepest level, monarchy—especially sacral monarchy—by being a truth embodied, achieves the perpetuation of the Mystery of the Incarnation in the temporal arena. By this mystery of royal theurgy, this incarnate blessing upon a nation, monarchy always stands as a living refutation and practical safeguard against the reign of egregores. If Europe is ever to become Christendom again, it will first need to be freed from the egregores that now control it, and the royal houses will thus have to play a central role in this deliverance.

---

[2] See my essay "Lost Dignity: On the Dignified Aspect of Government and the Problem of Totalitarianism," in Joseph Shaw, ed., *A Defence of Monarchy* (Brooklyn, NY: Angelico Press, 2023), 53–60.

8

CHRISTENDOM IS BENEDICTINE

THE philosopher Alasdair MacIntyre famously ended his 1981 masterpiece *After Virtue* by noting that the civilisational crisis in which the West has found itself, which the book explored with hitherto unseen erudition, needed "a new—doubtless very different—St. Benedict."[1] This observation inspired Rod Dreher, who went on to write the 2017 book *The Benedict Option*, a work that so captured the instincts of the awake minority about surviving in societies gripped by ideologies repudiating the whole Christian heritage that his book became a bestseller and was translated into many languages.[2] It is a book that deservedly will continue to be discussed for decades to come, and some of the observations and suggestions I make below are at least motivated by some of its themes. I want to suggest, however, that what we likely need isn't so new and different after all.

The appetite for a Benedictine-inspired response to the decay of late modernity is deeply attractive to me personally. My life has been bound up with the Benedictine charism since at least my teenagerhood. The first Catholic church I ever visited was that of Buckfast Abbey, on Dartmoor in England's deep west country. I was a young teen, and the experience changed me. It was the first time that I felt I was on ground that had not yet seen desecration. On that day, my father purchased for me an olive wood cross that one of the monks had

---

[1] Alasdair MacIntyre, *After Virtue: A Study in Moral Theory* (London: Bloomsbury, 2013), 305.
[2] Rod Dreher, *The Benedict Option: A Strategy for Christians in a Post-Christian Nation* (New York: Sentinel, 2017).

carved by hand, which now hangs above my marital bed. I cannot count the number of times I have returned to Buckfast Abbey, which remains a kind of spiritual home to me, and where I delight in praying before a special relic that is kept there: the hairshirt of that exemplary Benedictine oblate, St. Thomas More.

Some years after I first visited Buckfast, I was received into full communion with the Catholic Church while residing on the south coast of India, after having spent months living in a Benedictine Ashram founded by Swami Dayananda, better known as Dom Bede Griffiths, the student of C. S. Lewis who became a heterodox but brilliant Christian guru in Tamil Nadu. Later still, I proposed to the woman who became my wife on the steps of a Benedictine monastery. Over the years, I have delivered lectures at abbeys such as Norcia, Buckfast, Ampleforth, and Downside, the last of which generously paid me in jars of honey. I have visited the Baroque monasteries of Austria and the austere Gothic monasteries of northern Europe. I have basked in the glory of the almost Grecian temple-like monastery of Monte Cassino and I have vanished into the caves of St. Benedict's original retreat in the cliff at Subiaco. When I lived in Rome, I would take every opportunity to visit the Benedictine-run St. Paul Outside the Walls, in what is one of the Eternal City's grottiest districts; each time, it was as if I'd stumbled out of an alleyway in some American east-coast "ghetto" and into Gregorian Rome. Visiting monasteries is, I suppose, my habit.

Whenever I step foot onto Benedictine grounds, I feel as if I have come home. The chanting of the psalms, the sacrifice offered on the altars, the way of life lived under a Rule that's over a millennium and a half old—all the sacrality of these abbeys seems to have seeped into the stones themselves. Even after all the scandals, the collapse in vocations, and the ruination of the liturgy following that unhappy Vatican Council that baptised the fleeting fever of the 1960s—from which it will take many, many centuries for the Church to recover—the monasteries still appear as loci of divine grace, by which little parts of the diabolical principality we call the world has been captured and placed under Christ's kingship.

Some time ago, my family and I made a Lenten pilgrimage to Mount St. Bernard in Leicestershire, the only Cistercian Abbey in England (before Henry VIII's dissolution of the monasteries, there were forty-five Cistercian abbeys). Cistercians, being a reform of the Benedictines, follow the Holy Rule as faithfully as possible, and those at Mount St. Bernard bestow upon the faithful a great blessing by producing some of the very finest Trappist ale. Arriving at the Abbey, all the rush and hubbub of the modern world evaporates as one steps into a realm whose strict timetable of "prayer and labour"[3] appears to transcend time altogether.

The modern European finds himself dropped into existence with no clear sense of what came before and what will come after. He has no conception of being a link in an historical chain. He is utterly adrift. Trying to speak to the average modern about European identity is almost impossible. But if you try to coax him out of his slumber, the point of information on which I think you should begin is that Europe is, in essence, a creation of the Benedictine Order. If you can get the modern mind to understand *that*, then you have got quite far.

The Italian peninsula climbed out of the chaos of the Great Migration period in the early medieval age by the civilising effects of the Benedictine Order, which had been founded in Italy's mountains. King Clovis of the Franks was converted to the faith by his wife, St. Clotilde, who was herself educated by Benedictines, for whom she and Clovis later built the Parisian abbey of St. Genevieve. After the eradication of the Romano-British Church—which had its holy centre at Glastonbury—by

---

[3] One of many Benedictine mottoes is *ora et labora*, pray and work.

the incoming Northern European pagan tribes, England was reevangelised by Benedictines under St. Augustine, the Benedictine Archbishop of Canterbury who was sent to these isles by the Benedictine pope, St. Gregory the Great. The Germanic tribes were then evangelised by the English Benedictine monk St. Boniface, a mission later taken up by another Benedictine, St. Ansgar, "the Apostle of the North." In the next generation, another Benedictine, Adalbert of Prague, evangelised the Hungarians and Prussians. The charism of the father of Western monasticism proceeded to spread across the whole of Europe, with the old lands of the Roman Empire soon pulsating with the sacred chanting of monks everywhere.

After seven centuries of Islamic occupation, Spain was liberated. The Christian social order that was established there developed under the Benedictines initially sent from the great Abbey of Cluny following the Reconquista, and those "black monks" soon became the custodians of the Black Madonna at Montserrat. In the tenth century, after his baptism, Haakon the Good travelled from England to Scandinavia with the intention of converting the Norsemen to the True Faith, and for this purpose he took Benedictine monks with him.

For perhaps everything we associate with the great European tradition, we must be grateful to the Benedictines. Gothic architecture is an invention of the Benedictines, beginning with Abbot Suger's mesmerising initiative to incarnate his Neoplatonic ontology in stone and glass at St. Denis in Paris. Benedictine monks created the great libraries that preserved learning during the rampages of the Lombards, Goths, Saxons, Vandals, and all the other pagan barbarians who disdained humane learning quite as much as we do today. The universities grew out of the cathedral schools that were founded and led by Benedictines. And of course, the defence of Christendom—after two-thirds of the Christian world had been subdued by the forces of the crescent moon—was undertaken chiefly by the Knights Templar, the only equestrian order to adopt the Rule of St. Benedict, who ventured forth into the Holy Land against the Islamic foe.

There is almost nothing of our civilisation that cannot be in some way traced to the Benedictines. Indeed, the joys of my life—booze, hunting, education (treasured in that order)—are all connected with the Benedictine charism. It was the Benedictine monks at the Abbey of St. Hubert in the Lowlands who bred the famous St. Hubert hound, an ancestor of probably all European scent hound breeds. Some, of course, may say that it is an exaggeration to claim that Europe was an *invention* of the Benedictine Order. Even if I were to concede that it's an exaggeration—which I do not—it is certainly not an exaggeration to say this of Britain. The Benedictines gave to Britain in general, and certainly to England in particular, its unique spirituality. Many of our bishops and archbishops were Benedictines, from St. Dunstan who wrote the British coronation ceremony that not long ago captured the world's attention with the anointing of King Charles III, to St. Anselm, the first scholastic. And as it happens, the English Congregation is the oldest branch of the Order of St. Benedict in the world.

The traditional home of English Benedictine spirituality, and the ancient sanctuary of English Christianity, established by St. Joseph of Arimathea himself, is of course Glastonbury, where it is said that the abbey was one of the glories of all Christendom. Deep below those hallowed walls—now mere ruins—lay the unquiet grave of King Arthur, whose spectral presence continues to haunt the English as we await his second reign.[4] The English have an especial attachment to their landscape,

---

[4] For a wonderful study on the importance of Glastonbury for the unique spirituality of Britain, see Hugh Ross Williamson, *The Flowering Hawthorn* (Waterloo, ON: Arouca Press, 2021; originally published in 1962).

and they unknowingly listen out for the pounding can-
ter thereon of Camelot's knightly brotherhood. This
attachment to the landscape may be the principal characteristic of Albion's offspring, and it is likely inherited
from the millennium of Benedictine spirituality that
animated the religiosity of these isles. Benedictines,
unlike Franciscans or Dominicans, do not take vows
of chastity and poverty, even if there is an expectation
that they live chastely and without possessions. Besides
a vow of obedience to the Holy Rule and their superiors,
Benedictine monks and nuns take two further vows of
"stability" and "the conversion of manners." They vow,
then, to remain in a specific place, never to leave it for
somewhere they might deem preferable, and to undergo
the slow, incremental process of interior conversion of
their habits in relation to others—their "manners"—for
the sake of the spiritual transformation of their monastery and by extension, the world. England was covered
in abbeys from north to south, east to west, of holy
people promising to live in just this way. These abbeys
completely changed the nature of this land, thus turning
it into a home pleasing to God and man.

Today, the hundreds of abbey ruins scattered about
the British landscape, and the polished descendants of
rapacious thugs who live in grand houses called "Abbeys,"
testify to this astonishing monastic history and the sad
end to which it arrived. Fitting it is, then, that nowadays
there is a Benedictine convent at Tyburn, the site where
so many sons and daughters of St. Benedict, alongside
other British Catholics, were hanged for their love of
the ancient Faith. The nuns at Tyburn, who moved to
the site in 1903, are consecrated to the Sacred Heart of
Jesus, a theological mystery derived from the mysticism
of the German Benedictine saints Gertrude the Great
and Mechthild of Hackeborn (the imagery of which
later became important symbols of counter-revolution
during the age of so-called Enlightenment).

The reason why Europe cannot shake off its Christianity without losing a sense of its identity is because it was and still is covered in monasteries. This is also why the English could never wholly accept Protestantism, and they had to settle for a weird Catholic-Protestant hybrid called Anglicanism, forcing themselves to adopt an array of theological contradictions which together they charmingly called "religious moderation." Over the years, the English carefully avoided being troubled by such eccentricities as religious conviction by avoiding the topic of religion altogether. The problem, of course, is that one cannot live among monasteries for a thousand years and then successfully be secular. The English, in turn, remain intensely religious, but today they express their religiosity by their commitment to the petty secular causes and sentimental utopianism which has now left them jaded and unable to do anything except lie down and be colonised by foreign populations.

Not discounting its unique history, England is a kind of distilled example of what has happened across much of the West. A deeper dive into changes suffered by the Church and the culture it sacralised is necessary to understand how monasticism waned among Latin Christians, and why the survival of the Christian West will likely require a revival of monasticism—and that is the focus of the next chapter.

9

THE FALL OF MONASTICISM AND THE RISE OF CLERICAL MANAGERIALISM

ONASTERIES are built to last not for decades or even centuries, but for millennia. A monastery is meant to remain *there* and make *that* place holy, and that is the reason why monasteries were so successful in the creation of Christendom. But consecrated life, or what the Church calls "religious life"—that is, life lived under special vows—underwent big changes. Those changes came about due to the adaptation of religious life in the face of moments of crisis. But in the long run, such changes probably had unhelpful consequences. The consequences to which I refer slowly changed the Christian Faith from the permanent *form* of a concrete and settled way of life, to a set of intangible ideas or propositions which one either agreed with or did not.

Historically, the first dramatic change, it seems to me, was the rise of the friars. The first friar orders, the Franciscans and Dominicans, founded by their namesakes at around the same time in the thirteenth century, arose in response to the re-emergence of Manichaean sects throughout Europe. These sects were gnostic, disruptive, and spreading fast. In response, wandering monks—that is, friars—appeared, and they began to win back the people.

The appearance of the friars marked a revolutionary change: these new "monks"—free from the vow of stability—no longer remained in monasteries. They did not stay in one place to transform the area in which they'd settled, consecrating it down the centuries. These friars were on the move, wandering and preaching, turning up in cities and then disappearing again years—sometimes months, or even weeks—later. They established lasting priories, but the friars moved between those priories constantly. The friars were to have no lasting attachment to a particular place and its surrounding landscape. What is more, rather than seeing this change in the Church as an unfortunate innovation necessitated by an unavoidable crisis, new celebrity friars—including someone as influential as St. Thomas Aquinas—argued that their way of life marked the perfection of *all* religious life, combining as it did both contemplative and active life, whereas monks were disadvantaged by being contemplatives alone, so Aquinas argued.[1]

By this change in the conception of a "consecrated person," the Church was set on a trajectory that largely helped to unravel its mission centuries later. The friars were not farmers, artisans, and traders; they were full-time missionaries. They would come, render the faithful orthodox with their preaching, and leave. In this way, the definition of the Christian tacitly changed from a "liturgical person" to a "person who accepts certain propositions." The Faith, without anyone noticing, slowly changed from the existential transfiguration of human nature and the ongoing transformation of human culture to a set of formulae requiring assent. In short, the threads of rationalism, which would later deconstruct the Church and her mission, were sewn into her most holy organ, namely the consecrated life of her religious orders.

The Church was now set on a course from which she never swerved: the role of monastic life slowly diminished in its importance and in its presence in the Western Church. The Council of Trent in the sixteenth century, addressing the crisis of the Protestant Reformation, doubled down on the notion that the Christian religion is in essence a catechetical enterprise. The rise of the friars had set the Church on the path of clericalizing religious

---

[1] See *Summa Theologiae* II-II, Q. 188, art. 6.

life, and now, with the emergence of Protestantism and the opening up of the New World, it was believed that an even newer kind of religious life was needed. In turn, beginning with St. Ignatius of Loyola and his rather novel—and in the long run, disastrous—conception of religious obedience,[2] the notion of a "clerical order" appeared, soon being replicated in other orders, such as the Redemptorists and the Passionists.

I do not see in these developments some deliberate conspiracy against monastic life in the West, and neither do I think that the founders of these orders were not true saints. Indeed, I have a deep affection for St. Francis of Assisi in particular, whose life and charism I have argued elsewhere in this very volume ought to be taken as a special example in our epoch for how to rebuild the Church. The rise of the friars and then the clerical institutes undoubtedly responded to genuine crises and achieved astonishing successes in a short amount of time. Nonetheless, with these innovations, the Church over time lost something, perhaps its noblest treasure; it lost its sense of the privileged place of monasticism in the establishment of Christian societies. And so too, slowly, the entire Church moved from a monastic culture to a clerical culture, and hence from a consecrated culture to a managerial culture, the consequences of which have not been good to say the least.

That great authority on monasticism, St. John Cassian, who so influenced St. Benedict, had been profoundly worried by the prospect of any clericalization of religious life. Indeed, Cassian wrote that when a bishop visited a monastery, the unordained members should literally hide themselves out of sight to avoid being ordained by the bishop during his visit. Thus, in his Rule, St. Benedict insisted that priesthood would have nothing to do with

---

[2] For a penetrating study of this matter, see John Lamont, "The Catholic Church and the Rule of Law," in Peter A. Kwasniewski, ed., *Ultramontanism and Tradition* (Lincoln, NE: Os Justi Press, 2023), 78–106.

a monk's station in the hierarchy of the monastery.[3] The Benedictine monastery was not to be a clerical institute but a community of Christian brothers under vows and a common rule. Today, however, the clericalization of religious life has so infected the Western Church that if you visit any Benedictine, Cistercian, or Trappist monastery, you will invariably find that *all* the monks are either priests or undergoing training for priesthood. And the notion that a lay brother of a monastery could become, say, an abbot is unthinkable. Undoubtedly St. Benedict— himself a lay brother who was never ordained—would have been deeply unimpressed.

With this clericalization of religious life, the orders of consecrated Christians were increasingly deemed mere extensions of the priestly hierarchy. These orders, however, had largely been founded on the initiatives of unmarried lay people. But gradually the Church's members forgot this. And by the time of the Second Vatican Council, a new ecclesiology had appeared in which it was held that there were now three states in the Church: the priesthood, laity, and religious. This is obviously false. Traditionally, the Church's constitution was deemed not tripartite, but bipartite, on the model of the Incarnation itself, of which the Church is the mystical extension and perpetuation. It was understood that there were two states ordinary to the Christian life, namely clerical and lay, corresponding to the divine nature and sacred humanity of the one person of Jesus Christ.

This, if you like, is the horizontal dualism of the Church: two states, clerical and lay, ordinary to Christians. These states had different roles; put crudely, the clerics were to sanctify the laity and the laity were to sanctify the world. Out of the ordinary states, however, Christians—clerical or lay—could be called into

---

[3] Chapter 62, in *The Rule of St Benedict in English* (Collegeville, Minnesota: Liturgical Press, 1981), 93–94. The point is also stressed in chapters 2, 60, and 63, so important was it to the holy legislator.

an *extraordinary* way of life properly called "religious," in which one enters the supernatural spousal condition of consecration. Thus, the Church's traditional ecclesiology recognised two sets of two states, horizontal and vertical: clerical and lay, and secular and religious. Secular Christians can be clerical or lay, and religious Christians can be clerical or lay. And religious orders may have consecrated or secular members, the former having taken vows and the latter being lay people or secular clergy—like diocesan priests, for example—who are traditionally called "tertiaries" or "oblates."

So, in the Church's traditional ecclesiology, members of either of the two ordinary states might be consecrated, having taken vows of religion, but by so doing they do not cease to be clerical or lay. But after the "new Pentecost" of the Second Vatican Council, consecration in religious life wasn't considered something that belonged to an *extraordinary* calling which could be offered by Christ to any Christian, clerical or lay, but rather it was judged another state altogether. The bipartite Christological constitution of the Church was done away with. And once we lost a sense of religious life as something distinct, as belonging to an extraordinary calling, we then started commonly using "vocation" to refer to any life choice. The notion of the special supernatural spousal calling of religious life—something *extraordinary*, not *ordinary*, to the baptised—evaporated.

With the inflated role of the bishop as a kind of corporate manager on steroids, advocated by the Council's bad ecclesiology, the consecrated religious were then seen as quasi-clerical bodies totally under the management of the hierarchy. Given that most male religious members were ordained anyway, it was difficult to see how they might assert the autonomy of their consecrated religious life.

At present, those *non*-consecrated members of orders— traditionally known as "oblates" or "tertiaries," who are either single or married lay people or secular clergy—are routinely and erroneously called "lay members" of orders. (It's especially difficult to see how diocesan clergy who are tertiary members of orders are "lay members.") This may all seem beside the point, but the implication is that all the unordained consecrated male members as well as the nuns are *not* considered "lay members." So, what are they, then? Well, in the eyes of Rome, they appear to be considered sort of "half-clerics." So confused is modern Catholic ecclesiology that few seem to notice that none of this makes any sense. The effect, though, is that *all* monks, friars, and nuns—all who are not so-called "lay members" (that is, lay tertiaries or oblates)—are now deemed mere extensions of the hierarchy and treated as such. In turn, Rome routinely interferes with their constitutions, absolves members of their vows, and usurps their properties. And most members of most orders are so clericalized that they do not see this as a problem, or an abuse of power. The entire situation would be laughable if it were not blatantly sacrilegious.

Through this process of clericalization, monasticism waned in the West. The orders of friars and the clerical institutes grew far more numerous, and there also grew an ecclesiastical culture of privileging the secular priesthood of the dioceses. In short, the whole Church grew clerical, and the word "Church" itself largely became identified with the priesthood alone (despite the fact that priests made up a tiny percentage of the Church's overall faithful, and still do).

It took centuries of secular ideology and intense coercion to make Europe apostatise, and secularisation was achieved with such difficulty largely because the powers of Satan that gained ascendancy in modernity had to battle against the very essence of the Old Continent itself, an essence begotten by the mystic veil of monastic life that was draped over it for millennia. On the other hand, it takes a Pentecostal preacher one day in a South American town to have the whole of its population abandon their Catholic faith and adopt his religion. Why? Because South America was evangelised by friars and clerics who came, preached, and went. Hence, the evangelisation was skin-deep, whereas what the new world needed was an evangelisation that reached the heart, that is, the kind of evangelisation that comes from centuries of monasticism.

Rather than an ongoing, settled, stable way of life, Christianity became largely an intellectual exercise, which at the most plebeian level amounted to the learning of certain prayers and the memorisation of abbreviated catechisms. Sacred place gave way to sacred idea, and with the corruption of the Church's mission into mere abstractions, the life of grace morphed into something analogous to ideology, as is demonstrated by Catholicism's success as an internet genre. Still, at least prior to the Second Vatican Council, parish priests had canonical rights to remain at their parishes throughout their lives, which even through the clericalization of the Church allowed for some stability in the practice of religion. This right, however, was abolished with the new conception of bishops as all-powerful ecclesiastical managers which arose with the fashionable but injudicious episcopal theology of that Council.

A major aspect of this development was the class transformation of European society, which in turn changed the class dynamic of the Church. In the Middle Ages, it was landed aristocracy that populated monasteries just as much as the peasantry, two social classes characterised by loyalty to place and locality. But as the bourgeois class swelled down the centuries, its members—who were characterised by their attachment not to place but to commerce, and possessed a managerial mentality rather than one formed by *noblesse oblige*—began slowly to populate the Church. In late modernity, the Church's supreme office, the papacy, got its first middle-class pope, when hitherto this office had been occupied only by nobles and peasants. Pope Paul VI had all the characteristics of a middle-class manager. He was a social climber with a sympathy for *tabula rasa* ways of governing. Just as the bourgeoisie, with their privileging of ideas over realities—and their pathological impulse, rooted in rationalism, to conform the latter to the former—had overseen every modern revolution, so too Pope Paul oversaw an analogous revolution in the Church. He reduced the sacred liturgy from a mystical conduit of grace expressed in a sacred language to a vernacularised, didactic exercise to entertain a new, educated population.

In times of political revolution, typically a bourgeois progressive takes control, calls into question the organicism of the polity, and then claims to create a new nation altogether out of a paper constitution, which he then enforces through a network of similarly bourgeois, servile collaborators. So, too, the same model unfolded in the Church of the 1960s. With the Council that John XXIII had left him, Pope Paul oversaw the creation of a new ecclesiology from new non-dogmatic documents, for a new Church with a new liturgical culture, all born from a "new Pentecost." Since then, the Church has continued to recruit the most unremarkable, bourgeois managers into its clerical ranks, and by so doing her culture has completely changed—by which I mean nothing complimentary.

To this day, the monastic and contemplative life is routinely attacked by those at the highest echelons of the Church, and a mediocre episcopal caste of stale administrators oversees decline whilst recurrently insisting that some new catechetical programme will solve the problem of the widespread crisis in faith induction and faith retention.[4] Ideas, always ideas, will get us out of the crisis, so they think. (I am not convinced, of

---

[4] See Mary Cuff, "Why is the Vatican Assailing Contemplative Life," *Crisis Magazine,* November 15, 2021, https://crisismagazine.com/opinion/why-is-the-vatican-assailing-contemplative-life.

course, that they really see the apostasy of the Church's members as a crisis at all.)

What these ecclesiastical managers will certainly *not* do is acknowledge the signs of life that *actually* exist in the Church. I am afraid to mention any examples by name, given that the Eye of Sauron in Rome has long scanned the panorama of the Church for any such signs of life which, on seeing, it has immediately sent orcs to destroy. I will say, though, that there is at this time a monastery in Italy where the monks strive for holiness under the Rule of their holy father St. Benedict. Those monks offer the ancient liturgy and chant the psalms in their rite's sacred language. Remarkable numbers of devoted faithful attend their liturgies. Many, many families and individuals have moved to live near the monastery. Others travel from all around the world to visit the monastery, some travelling once or twice every year to pray there and be blessed by this otherwise forgotten part of the peninsula.

Those monks at the Italian monastery to which I refer have seen something that others have not. They saw that what we needed in the modern age was *not* a new and very different St. Benedict, but more likely an old and very similar St. Benedict. We needed the Christian religion not understood as a catechetical exercise, but as the ongoing, incremental transfiguration of nature by grace. Now, before anyone accuses me of denying that the faith is propositional, let me be clear that I believe that the Christian faith requires assent to propositions of divine revelation just as I believe that friendship requires belief in truths about one's friend. Given that the reception of grace moves one from enmity with God to friendship with God (James 4:4), the analogy isn't an inappropriate one. But if one were to think that friendship consisted solely of accepting propositions about one's friend, rather than merely presupposing the acceptance of such propositions, one would have misunderstood what friendship *is*. Friendship is something lived and stable, and this is infinitely more the case in reference to friendship with God. And it is that lived and stable friendship with God, proper to all Christians, that monasticism presents to the world in concrete form.

There is a widespread assumption among Christians today that if you get a person to accept certain Christian propositions, he will live as a Christian. In this way, we are all Protestants now. This assumption, of course, is undergirded by a typically rationalistic attribution to ideas of a causal power that they do not actually possess. It may be true, if I may put it Hermetically, that esoteric transformation is prerequired by exoteric transformation. But then the reverse is true as well, for these are correlated transformations. "As above, so below," as the maxim of the *Emerald Tablet* goes. For example, it is obviously true to say that you cannot have peace in your marriage until you have peace in your heart, but it is equally true that you cannot have peace in your heart if you do not have peace in your marriage. And if the obviousness of this observation is not immediately clear to you, then you are likely severely under the spell of rationalism. What monasticism achieved in the formation of our Christian civilisation was the establishment of Christianity not as a set of abstract ideas over which we could argue on the internet, but the infusion of every aspect of daily life by Redemption as *living* truth.

We must recover the existentiality of Christianity. And for this reason, I am quite sure that if the future will see any renewal and revival of the Church—and hence of our civilisation—it will be by the Church resituating monasticism at the heart of its life and its mission, and treasuring it as such. And it is this rediscovery of the role of monasticism in the Church as the foremost antidote to the Church's ills that I explore in the next chapter.

10

THE CHURCH OF THE FUTURE MUST BE MONASTIC

M O D E R N technology has allowed for a remarkable change in our working habits. In the UK,
following the COVID hysteria, a considerable
percentage of the population now works from home
or remotely in part or in full. A special moment has
arisen in which many of us can more or less choose
what kind of life we want to live, and then order our
income-earning around that way of life rather than
ordering our way of life around an office to which we
must daily travel. This allows for a new opportunity in
"Benedict Option" living.

I am aware of several parishes where the traditional
Latin Mass is offered, despite Rome's longstanding official campaign against it. Many families have moved to
the surrounding areas of those parishes and now home-
educate their children together. Much of this has been
made possible by recent changes in working habits and
the proliferation of new communication technologies.
The families of these church communities are living
in something like a new Benedictine arrangement, but
it's the "new" part of it that's the problem, for they do
not have a stable monastic community around which
to establish their lives. It can all be swept away at any
moment. And I know of at least one traditionalist community where what took years of hard work by the laity
to establish was thrown into disarray and destabilised
in just a few months due to power struggles between
bickering clergy. This is the kind of thing that happens
when your Christian life does not subsist in an arrangement that was established for the centuries.

The Eastern Orthodox faithful are at a certain advantage in this regard. In their ecclesial communion, monasticism maintained its proper, privileged place. Thus,
Orthodox faithful routinely enjoy the stability of liturgical and spiritual life that has all but vanished among
Latin Christians. The Orthodox also kept their ancient
liturgy, and they didn't adopt the pitiful managerialism
under which the Roman Church now toils. Of course,
they have other instabilities and problems, very serious
problems, including their weakening of the indissolubil-
ity of marriage, their perennial caesaropapism, and the
recent Constantinople-Moscow schism that has divided
the Orthodox union, to name just a few.

My own view, for what it is worth, is that the respective problems of Eastern and Western Christianity will
never be resolved while—in disobedience to Jesus Christ's
express prayer to the Father (John 17:22)—the apostolic
Church persists as a body halved by enmity and obstinacy.
Of course, such reunification won't happen anytime soon,
since Pope Francis successfully set ecumenical relations
back at least about five centuries. With his document
Traditionis Custodes, Francis demonstrated that he could
(and would) suppress an apostolic rite of the Church if
he felt like it. Hence, as an Orthodox theologian explained
to me, Orthodox Christians would be mad to entertain
communion with Rome and thereby put their beloved
liturgy at risk of being trampled by a half-educated
gangster from the Andes or one of his successors.

Indeed, the Orthodox will likely never entertain the
prospect of reunification with us Latins until Pope Francis has been personally and publicly condemned by a
future pope, and there is also some explicit declaration
that papal power cannot be exercised for the destruction
of that which it exists to protect (it is astonishing that
this even needs to be said). And while I think that—if
the Lord does not come in majesty beforehand—such a
condemnation and doctrinal clarification probably *will*

eventually take place (given that the alternative is the utter implosion of the Church under the weight of the monstrosity which the papacy has grown into), it likely will not happen any time soon.

Moreover, the reunification of East and West will require the consumption of so much humble pie on both sides that, from what I can tell, the self-satisfied moderns who currently occupy the Church's higher offices simply do not have the appetite. In turn, when it comes to reunification of East and West, I will continue to pray for it, but I'm not going to hold my breath. Nonetheless, I *will* pray for it, because it *must* happen, for I fear that the western Church will never rediscover its greatest treasure, namely its monastic charism, and so free itself from the yoke of clericalism, if it does not heal itself and become with the Orthodox one Church sacramentally *and* canonically.

The reason it is so pressing that the Church undergoes a rediscovery of its monastic life is because, in the coming age, I think it is by this rediscovery that it will survive. And this brings me back to Rod Dreher's *The Benedict Option.* You see, I think that we should accept Dreher's proposal, acknowledging that Christians need to be in the world but not of it, an imperative that is paramount in an age such as ours. But I want to suggest that we take that proposal a little more literally: we do not simply need to be inspired by the story of St. Benedict and the Order he founded; we need an actual revival of *real* monasticism in the West. We need literal monasteries. And those called to consecrated life ought to be founding priories and monasteries in cheap places—in Britain, that would mean places like Carmarthenshire, Country Durham, and Dumfriesshire—where the faithful can buy land close by, home-educate their children together, and regularly have access to the ancient liturgy which is their birthright (beyond which the Church is rapidly dying anyway). Bishops should be supporting such initiatives, even—fancy that—initiating them.

As things stand, however, were such initiatives to appear, the bishops would likely move in to destroy them. Some years ago, a not dissimilar initiative appeared in Glastonbury. A small group of Benedictines established themselves where once stood Romano-Britain's Christian capital. The Bishop of Clifton, in whose diocese they were, did not much like the monks' preference for the ancient Roman Rite liturgy, and he took full advantage of Pope Francis's dislike of this liturgy to make any future for the Glastonbury monks impossible. They were forced to find refuge in France, where they now continue their life in the countryside of the Vendée.

The desire to maintain the post-Conciliar concordat with the unconverted world and its ideology of liberal progressivism, the inflated managerial power of the episcopacy, and the lack of lay temporal power to keep episcopal toerags in check, has coalesced to create an episcopal class who will seek out and destroy the slightest sign of life in the Church. This problem will not be changed until, with the rejection of the centralisation that it has undergone, episcopal and papal power is reduced to what it ought to be: the authority to teach the Catholic Faith, sanctify the faithful with blessings and sacraments, and govern the Church in accordance with subsidiarity.

As noted, a large part of the UK population now works remotely, wholly or in part, and the statistics are probably similar for other European countries and for the USA as well. There is therefore a chance for people to gather around monastic settlements, and thereby to begin a monastic-based reevangelisation. Such reevangelisation would not be based on the quick fix of some new catechetical programme, but on the slow and deliberate capture of a part of this world, rendering it pleasing to God. From a very similar initiative, the glories of the high medieval period—with all its cathedrals and universities—emerged out of the dark ages of the Great

Migration period. The still practising remnant in many places across the world is trying to build a counterfeit of what the Church once offered as the basic foundation for a stable Christian society. They are gathering, buying property near to one another, and home-educating their children together. But it is always unstable. It is time to reestablish that for real, with real monasteries, with real monks, who take real vows of stability.

Some may say that those times are not our times, and hence we need something "new" and "very different." I say that our times are much more like the dark ages than many realise, which of course is the assumption underpinning Dreher's Benedict Option proposal. Back then, as Europe was beginning to settle, the Cistercian Order was founded at Cîteaux in France by a small group of Benedictines who wanted to live the Holy Rule more faithfully. For years, though, they struggled to recruit people to their monastery. Then, one day, a young nobleman called Bernard arrived at the Abbey in Cîteaux with a whole entourage of family members whom he'd convinced to join him in an attempt, he said, to escape hell. Soon others joined him—his own father, his extended family, his friends—all becoming monks at Cîteaux or nuns elsewhere. Under the inspiration of St. Bernard and his followers, the Cistercian reform quickly spread across the whole of Europe and transformed the religious climate of the continent. Behold, it only takes one man in poor health and a few companions, and God can set the whole world ablaze. We must never underestimate how much God can ignite with just the tiniest ember.

The wonderful writer Paul Kingsnorth has opined that St. Benedict was "the man whose rule was designed to tame" monasticism and "to bring the cave Christians into line." The Benedictine charism, Kingsnorth thinks, institutionalised and rendered "too comfortable" the hitherto wild way of life lived by Christian monks, exemplified by the Irish saints in Kingsnorth's romantic account of Celtic Christianity.[1] In reality, however, the Celts soon adopted the Benedictine Rule—with the Cistercian reform in particular thriving in Ireland—largely because the Benedictine charism institutionalised monasticism in the best possible sense. It blessed the landscape and permeated the quotidian with the sacred, ultimately sacralising the secular all the way down. The Benedictine Order successfully created a stable Christian social order that persisted through dizzying civilisational flux, and by so doing allowed the transformative mystical life proper to Christianity to be not merely the spirituality of an elite few, but something accessible to many, many people—from peasant farmers to emperors.

Today, in the entirely secularised West, there is no shortage of people longing for a public, "institutionalised" expression of religiosity. The saddest and most chaotic expressions are found in ritualistic wokeness, from Gay Pride to Extinction Rebellion; more edifying examples are found among the flocks of dreadlocked westerners who travel to Indian ashrams each year. The antithesis of the liberal privatisation of religion is the Benedictine consecration of the landscape and its seasons, in which all nature is assumed into the liturgical rhythm of the Church. And anyone who thinks that the Benedictine charism is "tame" not only has ignored the many Benedictine missionaries who wandered into unknown lands to contend with barbarians, often unto martyrdom, but needs also to study the near-psychoactive meditations of the Sibyl of the Rhine, Abbess Hildegard von Bingen, or read Abbot Johannes Trithemius's practical angelology of incubatory spellcasting. If it's an untamed "weird Christianity" that appeals to Westerners today, then the Benedictines were already there centuries ago.[2]

---

[1] Paul Kingsnorth, "A Wild Christianity," *First Things*, March 2023, www.firstthings.com/article/2023/03/a-wild-christianity.
[2] See Tara Isabella Burton, "Christianity Gets Weird," *New York Times*, May 8, 2020, www.nytimes.com/2020/05/08/opinion/sunday/weird-christians.html.

My preoccupation with monasticism is really to make one very simple point, and make it continuously in different ways. The point is that, even if the diagnosis of MacIntyre in *After Virtue* is correct—and I don't doubt the diagnosis—perhaps we do not need a new and very different St. Benedict. Maybe we need an old and very similar St. Benedict. We need monasteries. We need men and women consecrated to God, to vow to be obedient to their rule, convert their habits from those of modernity to those of grace, and stay put in the place in which they are. In short, we need nothing novel, fresh, innovative, or anything at all consonant with such unpleasant adjectives. We need old-fashioned, traditional Benedictines, and we need them everywhere. Without a stable Christian life, there is no Christian living. That is how the Church of the future will survive the looming dark ages, just as it survived the last dark ages: by the daily prayer and labour of the sons and daughters of St. Benedict.

11

ON KILLING OUR ELDERS

MANY years ago, aged nineteen, I travelled alone out of Kathmandu where I had been living as a bum for some months, my destination being the ancient temple complex of Bhaktapur. On the way, my tuk-tuk driver stopped at a small settlement to buy some bottled water. As I refreshed myself with a cold drink, I looked around at the little village beyond the staring faces of gathering residents. I decided that Bhaktapur could wait a day; I wanted to stay the night there in that village. With the locals, I communicated with big smiles, positive sounding noises, and the universal sign for "good": giving a thumbs-up. Soon, my tuk-tuk driver was heading back to the capital without me, and I had found somewhere to sleep. Some villagers led me up a hill at whose foot their primitive buildings were strewn. A little way up, I was brought to a small hut wherein the elders sat.

Perched on the floor, chatting away in hushed tones, were a group of elderly people. Together, we drank butter tea. They smiled. I smiled. I nodded my head up and down and they nodded—or rather, wobbled—their heads from side to side. Then, honour having been satisfied, we descended to the village for the night, where I slept on a semi-covered bench, leaving for Bhaktapur the following morning. What I have reflected on many times since that day was the immediate need felt by the young villagers to present me to their elders. The elders were, in that place, the heart of the community.

No traditional community has ever existed without an internal community of elders. In fact, we modern Westerners may be the first people in history to attempt to flourish without such a community. We place the elderly in "homes" to be cared for—and often, it has been discovered, abused—by foreign arrivals dressed up as healthcare professionals. The ethic of the "self-discovering individual" leaves no room for elders, who are increasingly discussed as either a potential or a real burden, especially by those who are themselves entering that time of life which would have, in a traditional society, placed them among the elders.

In a traditional society, the elder is a source—a treasury, even—of social and communal knowledge that allows a given community to live in a way that is contiguous with their ancestors. That is, the elder is a bridge between the generations down the centuries that conserved and protected the community against all odds, and those generations' living beneficiaries. Put another way, the elder both represents and embodies everything from which modern man seeks to emancipate himself. Hence, modern society not only has no place for the elder, but it must actively pursue the elder's disappearance, either by making him perpetuate his youth through cosmetics and technology, becoming by steps a freak of nature; or by hiding him away in a care home; or increasingly by developing the necessarily sophisticated and sophistical arguments to justify murdering him with "dignity."

In traditional societies, elders are deemed to possess knowledge of the *actual* community within which they live. They offer some parting guidance by which those who are undergoing the initiatory rites to enter the community, or those who are now leaders in the community, may increase their practical wisdom. Elders have what is called "ancestral knowledge." This knowledge is typically neither very conceptually abstract nor technical, but narrative-based, prudential, and experiential. They needn't have any special qualification or professional status. They are treasured by virtue of their years. Elders are frequently story tellers and patient listeners. Most importantly, elders might not be able to say much about "man," but they will be able to say a lot about "Tom" or "Harry." That is to say, elders know the members of their community, and they know that what might work for Tom likely won't work for Harry, and so they can nudge people this way or that when giving counsel because they know with whom they're dealing.

This kind of knowledge—the knowledge of years—is, practically speaking, the most important knowledge to access in the raising of new generations, if indeed the *flourishing* of those generations, and not their mere *use*, is the primary objective of the whole community. We, of course, do not place such weight on this kind of knowledge. This may seem strange, but it really is extremely important to understand that modern man is not like his antecedents. He does not simply instantiate an organic, historical development continuous with those of previous generations; he is something quite new.

Go into any old church or cathedral in Europe and you will typically see at least one image of the crucifixion of Jesus Christ. In the image, you will see men and women standing around the foot of the cross: the women who wept there, the beloved disciple, a mounted Roman soldier, and likely non-Biblical characters like a saint to whom there was a local devotion, or a rich merchant or nobleman who was the artist's patron and therefore paid for the fresco. You will see that all the people in the image are in the garb of the time in which the image was painted. If it is medieval, everyone depicted will be dressed as medieval Europeans. If the image is from the Quattrocento, everyone will be in clothes typical of the European Renaissance. And this habit of painting everyone in the garb of the day remained the case for works of art until the birth of modernity in the eighteenth century.

How is it that depicting the crucifixion of Jesus Christ surrounded by people in the present-day dress of the artist did not seem ridiculous to him, his contemporaries, and indeed does not appear ridiculous to us now? For just imagine if we tried to do the same thing. Imagine an artist today depicting the crucifixion scene with the Roman soldiers in commando camo and bulletproof vests, the Virgin grieving in a navy trouser suit, St. John comforting her while outfitted in trainers, sweatpants, a hooded jumper, and his favourite Nike t-shirt. Such an image would likely be considered one of three things: either a bad joke, a gimmick by a failing artist, or propaganda art of the cringeworthy sort used by Jehovah's Witnesses in their *Watchtower* magazine.

The reason why our ancestors in each premodern age could depict themselves, the saints, and the biblical characters standing upon Calvary in contemporary dress is because they saw themselves as belonging to the same civilisation as that whose genesis began on that very hill—and so they did. That is, they held the story given to them in Holy Writ and their own story to be the same story. We moderns, on the other hand, even those who believe in the Christian religion, cannot help but look at the religious deposit that actuated our civilisation as the cult of an alien species.

"Modernity" is merely the term for that time in history that is both intellectually and practically devoted to atheism in its various ideological forms. Modernity is, at the deepest level, a break with everything prior to it, for everything prior to it was intensely religious. Unfortunately, by being thus devoted to atheism, modernity possesses neither meaning nor purpose. In turn, our civilisation is rapidly collapsing and the alienation that modern man experiences—from himself, his neighbour, and his world—is intensifying at a rate that makes the approaching decades look very alarming. And through this process of "biting our chains," as Edmund Burke put it, we are now drifting into the abyss.[1] Amid such

---

[1] Edmund Burke, "Speech on the Impeachment of Mr Warren Hastings," quoted in Robert Lindsay Schuettinger, *The Conservative Tradition in European Thought* (New York: G. P. Putnam's Sons, 1970), 47.

a process of entirely breaking with the past, there is no place for the elder—who is, as it were, the very chain that is being bitten.

As the example of sacred art indicates, the one institution that ought to be able to affirm the role of the elder is the Church. The Church, in fact, lives by reverence for elders. Sacred Scripture is the story of the patriarchs, the apostles, and the disclosing of a Father-God. The Church's theology is orthodox only insofar as it does not depart from the doctrine of the Church Fathers. The Church, both clerical and lay in its constitution, *is*, if you like, the society in which the charism of the elder is supernaturalised and rendered sacred and sacrosanct.

Tragic it is, then, that the Church's current hierarchical incumbents seem, generally speaking, to be neither elders themselves nor to love *their* elders. They appear as frustrated rascals who have undergone all the humane development and civilisational induction of Tolkien's orcs. Perhaps this ought not to surprise us. After all, the men who fill the Church's higher offices today were all formed in the crucible of the Second Vatican Council's progressive theology, and their intellectual habits were fashioned by daily exposure to the so-called liturgical "reform." The "experts" who subjected the Church's liturgical heritage to ongoing experimentation did so on the grounds that it was somehow legitimate to call into question—and redact or even reject altogether—huge swathes of prayer and mystical experience inherited from our ancestors in religion, the sum total of elder-wisdom in ritual form. The very Council, then, that claimed power to renew the Church's youth in fact emptied the churches, and by so doing it aged the Church rapidly, in turn aging the civilisation she once animated, as Valentin Tomberg observed.[2] And this process of aging the Church, far from recovering her charism as the Great Elder of our civilisation, merely rendered her decrepit.

---

[2] See Tomberg, *Meditations*, 294.

Some years ago, during one of Pope Francis's flashy and since-forgotten events in Rome, the Filipino Cardinal Tagle had a video made of himself for YouTube. There, he can be seen dancing and apparently pretending to be a rapper. It makes for very uncomfortable watching. The important thing about the short video is that Tagle says the following words:

> You young people have taught me, have taught the elders, valuable lessons about humanity and about following Jesus. And I hope you will continue teaching us, and I also hope that we elders could have something to teach you. So, let us journey together in this common path of becoming a better Church and a better world.

Nice sentiments, to be sure, but the entire video's style makes it clear that he has little or nothing to say to the modern world that isn't affirming of its trajectory. All Tagle and those like him can say—as "elders"—is that the whole paradigm of breaking free from our elders is one filled with justified optimism. Tagle, in that video, swaying to a synthetic beat in the cardinalatial garb that is meant to evoke the call to martyrdom, looks as ridiculous as St. John the Divine dressed in a tracksuit.

Such a spectacle is especially depressing in the case of a churchman, but its likeness is replicated across wider society. Even those who could—by some great conversion of the public arena—now become society's elders, namely today's Boomers, have so bought into the paradigm of elder-killing and the imperative to seek eternal youth through perennial moral emancipation, that they literally cannot *be* elders. In the Lord's dialogue with Nicodemus (John 3:1–21), two paths are presented to us: the path of forever seeking the return to your mother's womb, and the path of the Spirit. The former leads you to become spiritually childish, and the latter spiritually childlike. Between those two conditions of soul is the void between hell and heaven. The perpetual search for the mother's womb, however, is the one chosen by our epoch, a childish quest to flee reality which we are now grotesquely pursuing through the coalescing technologies which belong to virtual "reality" and transhumanism.

As happens in every instance of modernity's break with nature and tradition, we haven't actually got rid of that from which we have sought to emancipate ourselves, but only replaced it with a degraded version of the same thing. We got rid of indissoluble marriage, as it was understood by our ancestors, and we have since created a whole industry of soulmate-finding. We got rid of childhood innocence, and now we've created an entire entertainment industry based on perpetuating childish fantasies. We destroyed concrete and local communities and now we seek to join an ever-growing number of "online communities." We threw out liturgical religion and have since largely created the modern world by way of pseudo-liturgical spectacles.[3] Modernity is characterised by the tragic and desperate attempt to emancipate ourselves from that for which we immediately make a rubbish counterfeit.

This pattern of replacing what we had with a poor version of the same thing is clearly observable in the cultural killing of our elders, for our societies are now full of therapists and counsellors. Thus, we moved from treasuring an internal community of people with experiential knowledge and a love for those who seek their counsel, to contracting professionals with technical knowledge who do not want to "bring their work home with them." We went from a people who will seek a solution for the problems that arise, for love of the community that they helped to build, to a people in whose financial interest it is to perpetuate the problems encountered. The very stupid assumption behind this

---

[3] Modern ideologies—like liberalism, fascism, communism, and newer forms of progressivism—are "performative" in many ways, offering counterfeit ritual for the given ideological regime and its social paradigm. "Pride Month" is the most obvious current example of this in the West.

shift from the elder to the therapist—an assumption
so typical of modern man—is that in some way it is
possible to bypass experience and the accumulation
of practical wisdom by the accrual of qualifications.
And hence, *despite* experience, people irrationally place
their emotional development and their life's future in
the hands of a stranger for no other reason beyond a
thoughtless prejudice in favour of so-called "experts."

Sadly, that kind of stupidity has its analogue in the
Church, too. It is disheartening to see how vulnerable
Christian faithful, especially women, gather round a
newly ordained priest as if he is some kind of oracle
who can, at the drop of a word, transform the lives of
those who dote on him. This error is in fact the same as
the error that causes people to place themselves in the
hands of therapists, but only this time with a religious
veneer. Whereas in the former example, the therapist is
thought to bypass experience and embodied knowledge
by way of a qualification, the young priest is thought
to do so by way of his ordination. It is thought that,
somehow, whatever he has received by supernature isn't
going to transform his nature but circumvent it altogether. This inversion of Christian anthropology, which
supposes that some "special grace" can aptly substitute
for the unfolding of human experience *in time*, comes
from the kind of abstractionism that is the hallmark of
the modern mind. Thus, one can see how what often
passes for traditional Christian piety and obedience
might be nothing more than the deleterious assumptions
of modernity masquerading as true religion.

For me, the paradigmatic example of modernity's
elder-killing was the one I witnessed in the life of Roger
Scruton. Scruton was a man who had throughout his life
coupled an outstanding intellectual search with the concrete experience that allowed his knowledge to take the
form of wisdom. When he spoke, those around him fell
silent. During the four years I regularly met with him as

his research student, I knew I was enjoying the great for-
tune of spending time with a man who was offering his
accumulated wisdom to a people he loved, whose future
he worried about. In short, Scruton was a true elder.

In April of 2019, George Eaton, a snivelling little runt
with the vacant eyes of someone for whom integrity
is mysterious, pretended that he wanted to conduct a
sincere interview with Scruton for *The New Statesman*,
only later to misrepresent what Scruton had said. Given
that most of my readers will know this very unedifying
story, it's not worth retelling in entirety here. In any
case, Scruton was later vindicated thanks to the jour-
nalist Douglas Murray obtaining a true recording of the
original interview. But that was not before Scruton's
health had been severely affected due to the public
attack first by Eaton and then by the cowardly Tory
MPs who fell over each other to denounce a man who
was a thousandfold their better. That Eaton is still able
to work in journalism to this day is an indication of
the general corruption of our era.

The point is that what played out in those events
was a distillation of the emancipator-elder dichotomy of
modernity. Eaton went to Scruton's London apartment
with the intention of killing one of society's great elders,
not physically but morally and socially. And that story,
half a decade later, ought to have become for those
who care about our civilisation something of a parable,
or at least a cautionary tale. That is to say, we need to
decide what kind of society we want to live in: one in
which the Eatons of this world have the upper hand,
or the Scrutons. Put differently, do we want to live in
a society in which we must all fear destructive little
toerags—that is, the kind of society we currently live
in—or one that treasures its elders?

Of course, the process of killing our elders is not new.
For decades now, parents have sought to sever their offspring from the civilisational inheritance into which they

should have inducted them. Neither of my parents were christened when they were babies. My father requested to be baptised in early teenagerhood and my mother in early adulthood. The traumatised generation that had suffered the bloodbaths of the twentieth century wanted to free themselves and their children from all the history that had led up to those conflicts, when in fact those wars were the supreme creations of modernity, its final birth pangs.

Indeed, the process of killing our elders began long ago, and whether we can escape that process now is one for which the jury is still out. What we *can* do, however, is reject it in our own homes—at least for now, until the "mortal god" of the modern state finds new technological means to regulate more closely the domestic sphere. I want my children to sit attentively at the feet of their grandparents, as if they have something to learn, because they do. Indeed, I want to be unchildish enough to offer something to my grandchildren when my children grow up, marry, and have their own offspring. And at this juncture in history, I can think of an attitude no more restorationist, reactionary, and counter-revolutionary than that.

12

START YOUR DAY LIKE A KNIGHT TEMPLAR

AS the reader will have gathered by now, I prop-agate an intensely incarnational spirituality, and as noted, one of the ways by which the great, incarnational, Benedictine charism has been lived in past ages was through the knightly code of the Templar Crusaders. Now, I submit that part of the incarnational spirituality that I defend might be that of exercising just like a Crusader. My neighbours have in fact grown accustomed to seeing me each morning in my garden, moving about in nothing but my underpants whilst wielding a heavy metal mace to the chants of Hildegard von Bingen. They probably found it alarming initially, but there I am almost every morning, nearly naked, clubbing imaginary Saracen invaders. Seeing me there is as predictable as the sun rising.

Being a writer and researcher, it is very difficult to keep fit. I walk my dog a couple of times a day and I hunt through the Season, but most of my life is seden-tary. This inactive existence is especially problematic for I am racked with back problems, including scoliosis, the effects of which can only be kicked down the road by the strengthening of core muscles and constant move-ment. Not good, then, for a bookish sort. And I do not want to be crippled by my poor spine too early, as for many years to come I hope to lift my children into my arms and charge about with them, I want to be able to haul a freshly shot buck up a hill, and in the decades to come I want to dance at my children's weddings.

When it came to regular exercise, I tried everything. I sprinted. I used dumbbells. I used kettlebells. I used resistance bands. I used an outdoor gym. But nothing quite seemed to build up the core strength that I needed. Then, one day, searching about online, I learned that some Westerners were turning to a fitness tool that had been used for three millennia by Persians and Indians both for cardiovascular endurance and core to upper body strength: the gada.

A gada is what in English we would call a mace. It is a stick with a heavy ball on the end. In India, this weapon is associated with Hanuman, a monkey-god especially venerated by Indian wrestlers who have been using gadas for as long as history to build up their throwing power. In the last couple of decades, the traditional Indian gada has been developed by Western fitness enthusiasts into a sleeker piece of equipment simply called a "steel mace."

There are a set number of movements that one must first learn in order to wield a steel mace effectively and gain the most from one's morning workout: 360s, 8-10s, front presses, grave diggers, uppercuts, barbarian squats, hand switches, joust lunges, jabs, rows, and a few more. Once you know these, and you've practised them to the point that you're confident in executing them without injuring yourself, it then gets really interesting. Interesting, because you can then integrate these movements into a seamless single complex which looks like something between a martial arts *kata* and a dance. Throw the Sybil of the Rhine's mystic chants into the mix and you have there a pretty enrapturing start to the day.

Continuous movement with a mace over a prolonged period of time is referred to as "mace flow," a phrase that seems fitting as its practice quickly places one into what psychologists call the "flow state." The flow state is a temporary cognitive disposition in which one is so immersed in the activity at hand, and so concentrated on the task—which is crucial during mace training, for the alternative to intense concentration is hitting oneself with a large ball of solid steel—that one ceases to see from without, so to speak. Such a shift in perception is no small achievement, for the modern mind is an observing mind and not a participatory mind. The observing mind is a mind a step removed from reality, rather than in union with it. And it is precisely our proclivity for observing everything, rather than becoming mentally absorbed in reality, that not only makes our observation so blind but ever escalates our modern sense of alienation, from each other and from the world.

Perhaps worse than our alienation from each other and from the world around us, however, is the alienation modern man feels from his very own body. Increasingly, psychologists are linking widespread depression to the deficit of embodied "flow" in modern life. This problem is made worse by the proliferation of counterfeit flow experiences found in videogames, in which one experiences all the concentration without any of the embodiment essential for feeling alive. The result is dejection and frustration. At the end of a mace workout, on the other hand, one feels exhausted but fully alive. Moving to the rhythm of the music while an ancient weapon soars around your body mentally places you in an experience of the ages, in which the spirits of all the great warriors down the centuries are incarnated in your activity.

Generally speaking, there are two types of people who are interested in mace training: new agers and neo-vikings, between whom you can only fit a Rizla paper in any case. This is perhaps understandable, as members of both groups would typically look a little out of place in a commercial gym. Both groups are veiled traditionalists, who instinctively look for manifestations of traditional cultures and ancient wisdom traditions as sources of meaning. Both groups also privilege belonging over vanity, which is why they tend to build strong communities of people who look awful.

Since I was introduced to this marvellous figure of history, when mace training I like to recall the French knight Jean II Le Maingre "Boucicaut" (1366–1421)—widely deemed the personification of chivalry and a knight perhaps unequalled in his number of campaigns—whose biographer in a work written during Boucicaut's lifetime had this to say about him:

> He would train for hours with a battle-axe or a hammer to harden himself to armour and to exercise his arms and hands, so that he could easily raise his arms when fully armed. Doing such exercises gave him a physique so strong that there was no other gentleman in his time who was so proficient—for he could do a somersault fully armed but for his bascinet, and he could dance equipped in a coat of mail.

That is what is especially enjoyable about using a mace: one feels like a warrior in training. And on account of the countless hours I have spent wielding what is essentially an ancient weapon of war, I feel that I could confidently defend myself with a cudgel—and when one is under attack, most nearby objects look a lot like a cudgel.

A great thing about the mace is that all you need is this one exercise tool, which can be stored easily, and which prioritises not vanity but functional strength training that focuses on the core muscles. In *The Road to Wigan Pier*, George Orwell writes of going down a coal mine and watching the men strip off to work in the muggy conditions there, and he notes that he'd been hitherto unaware that human bodies could be so beautiful. Those men did not have bulging vanity muscles like those that exercise machines can give you, but they had the bodies of men who *move*.

When using a mace, you are contending with an offset weight, which means that as it moves it constantly destabilises you, requiring you to engage your

stabilising muscles to stay upright. This in turn builds
the muscles you need to move quickly, it gives you a
good posture, and it affords you a certain control over
your body that otherwise is easy to lose. The mind's
union with the body is an aspect of human existence
that ought to concern us, given that its disunion with
the body is the very definition of death. And death
doesn't just come all at once, it creeps up on you. Men
in particular should be aware of this; for as men age,
their testosterone levels rapidly drop—and modern men
have a bad start anyway due to the oestrogen-mimicking
isoflavones in processed foods and the contraceptive pill
in the tap water—and then they get weaker, get sick
more frequently, and their cognition slows down. But
men can impede this process, even reverse it, and one
way to do that is by a hundred barbarian squats with
a heavy mace every other morning.

Ironically, given the name of the exercise, barbarian
squats with a heavy mace every other morning may
need to be part of our repertoire as we attempt to flee
the barbarism of late modernity. For in the West, the
mace is a symbol of civilisation. In particular, maces
symbolise jurisdiction and power. Maces are displayed
in parliaments to indicate that they are in session and
are fully constituted. In the UK, the parliamentary use
of the ceremonial mace specifically symbolises the role
of the Crown, and the fact that the government gathered there is so gathered as the monarch's government.
Maces are carried before liturgical processions, marching
military troops, and the chancellors and academic staff
of universities—the last of these to indicate the inde-
pendence and authority of such treasuries of wisdom,
as they once were. Hence, maces are, in our civilisation,
always present at its sources, and they should remain in
our minds symbols of the marvellous but fragile culture
we have established together, against all odds, down the
centuries—and thus its need to be defended.

The kind of men who want to build civilisations, men like the ancient Athenians or the medieval nobility, must not only dedicate themselves to worship and study, but they must train. Civilisation-builders should both *look* and *be* strong, as if prepared for anything. It is worth remembering that no one knows what is around the corner. Had you told me in 2019 that we would all soon be thrown under house arrest and threatened with loss of employment if we did not take experimental gene-therapies, I would not have believed you. Had you told me in 2020 that Eastern Europe would soon be cast into an internal war, I would have at least had my doubts. History has no direction, and nothing can be reliably predicted. Take control, then, over those few things that you *can* control. Get fit, get strong, and get close to God. Move around your garden or your living room, half-naked, wielding a steel mace for forty minutes each morning whilst listening to chant. There is no better way to begin your day, or to prepare for tomorrow.

APPENDIX 1
A Correspondence with Peter Kwasniewski on Grace, Vocation, and the Modern Church

LETTER 1

Dear Sebastian,

My wife and I, both Benedictine oblates, have enjoyed your reflections on Benedictine monasticism. Your views and mine coincide to a very great extent. Norcia is the place in Europe I have visited the most—easily a dozen times by now. I attended a Benedictine high school and have worked in an academic capacity for Benedictine monasteries. I go on retreat in Gower, Missouri, with the Benedictines of Mary.

We are birds of a feather. Like you, I see rationalism as the key issue, and your argument that the mobility and impermanence of the friars and the clericalism fostered by later clerical orders contributed to a certain kind of rationalism whereby Christianity was seen more as propositional assent than as a way of life is certainly compelling. But the friars themselves, and later the clerical orders of the Counter-Reformation, also promoted a grand liturgical life, built magnificent churches of their own, developed forms like the oratorio and the cantata; theirs was a creative outpouring and outreach such as few periods of the Church have ever seen. The monasteries were never meant to accomplish those goals, which seemed peculiarly suited to the rise of great cities where monasteries would usually not be at home. And certainly, we owe the codification (I would prefer to say "canonization") of the ancient Roman Rite in its medieval plenitude to a Dominican pope, Pius V.

I think you should give Urban Hannon's (helpfully compact) book, *Thomistic Mystagogy*, a close look.[1] He makes a compelling case for St. Thomas as very much in line with the medieval allegorical-spiritual tradition of liturgy, making him far more monastic, on your account, than mendicant. Of course, Thomas was educated as a child oblate at Montecassino, so it makes sense. True, he did defend the mixed contemplative-active life, as you said, but there are tensions in Aquinas on that topic, just as there are tensions in Aristotle about whether the philosophical or the political life is higher; and Aquinas, in his more Augustinian moments, defends contemplation as the highest activity and *telos* simply speaking (certainly that is true in heaven!).

A more substantive disagreement concerns the modern opinion that St. Benedict was not a presbyter. Cardinal Schuster devotes many pages in his illuminating *Saint Benedict and His Times* to explaining why all of the evidence points to the saint's having been a priest.[2] Moreover, it is not clear at all to me that the medieval trend toward ordaining "choir monks" as priests in order to perfect their daily offering of the *sacrificium laudis* through the so-called "private Mass" is necessarily to be seen as a negative "clericalization." The Cluniac emphasis on the daily round of prayer, both communal and individual, long predated the mendicant orders and clerical orders that followed, and very much relied on a robust army of lay brothers, preserving that double complexion (clerical and lay) on which you rightly place emphasis.

I applaud the following crisp statement: "The clerics were to sanctify the laity and the laity were to sanctify the world." That is almost a one-line summary of my

---

[1] Urban Hannon, *Thomistic Mystagogy: St. Thomas Aquinas's Commentaries on the Mass* (Lincoln, NE: Os Justi Press, 2024).
[2] See Ildephonse Schuster, *Saint Benedict and His Times* (Waterloo, ON: Arouca Press, 2021).

book Ministers of Christ: Recovering the Roles of Clergy and Laity in an Age of Confusion.[3] Well, to be accurate, I also spend a good deal of time defending the traditional minor orders as part of the ancient and necessary ecclesiastical hierarchy.

We are in agreement about the abuse of the term "vocation," and in fact I have in the past advanced a similar argument to yours.[4] Moreover, your critique of churchly managerialism is the best I've ever seen, and your continued refrain that we need, not a very different Benedict, but the same one, doing the same kind of thing—obedientia, stabilitas loci, conversio morum—is rhetorically very effective, as the repetition subtly imitates the very ideas you are advocating: obedience to a rule, staying in one place and loving it and sacralizing it, and turning around one's manners to conform to the model.

Do you know about the unfortunate Hilarion Heagy? He was first a Russian Orthodox priest, after that an Eastern Catholic priest, and then he renounced Christianity to embrace Islam. Reading him, I am put in mind of such figures as Frithjof Schuon, René Guénon, Titus Burkhardt, men who also ended up with... Islam. While I respect the theological and mystical writings of certain Islamic authors, I find the decisions of these "perennialists" extremely baffling. Giving up Christ, the Logos Incarnate, would be impossible for me, regardless of how bad things get in the Church.

In any event, I was struck by something Heagy wrote a few days ago on his blog:

> By their fruits you shall know them (Matthew 7:16).
> In many ways, this was my criteria. What are the

---

[3] Peter Kwasniewski, The Ministers of Christ: Recovering the Roles of Clergy and Laity in an Age of Confusion (Manchester, NH: Crisis Publications, 2021).

[4] See Peter Kwasniewski, "There's an essential difference between the calling of the laity and a religious vocation," LifeSiteNews, February 2, 2021, www.lifesitenews.com/blogs/theres-an-essential-difference-between-the-calling-of-the-laity-and-a-religious-vocation/.

fruits, as I see them first hand? Admittedly by 2022, I was thoroughly battered by much that I had experienced in the Church—even as I tried to give myself completely to the service of an institution that seemed increasingly disinterested in its own survival. Instead, it seemed to me like "the world"—the *dunya*—was the main focus of much of Christianity. Or simply politics. This, coupled with a loss of tradition—of objective tradition and of a deeper esoteric tradition—and an increasingly totalitarian stranglehold of the subjectivity in Christianity (i.e., "my truth," "my belief," "my 'special' relationship," "my reality," "my understanding"...etc.) Well...I saw everywhere I looked no real unity, but rather a cacophony of chaos.

This very much reminded me of some themes in your writing. Thank you, as always, for your immensely stimulating work.

In Domino,
Peter

LETTER 2

Dear Peter,

Thank you so much for your kind remarks and thoughtful criticisms of my writings on Benedictine monasticism and its spirituality. I certainly do not deny the advantages that you highlight regarding the development of religious life over the centuries in the Latin Church, but I *do* hold that such development entailed in the long run an obscuring of Catholic religious life and what religious consecration actually *is*. That development—from monasticism to the rise of the friars, and from the friars to the clerical institutes—has I think some important explanatory power for understanding how we ended up with the dominant culture we now have in the Catholic Church, namely a culture of clericalism.

Moreover, whilst I agree with you that the later orders were able to embark on "outreach" that the monasteries could not, I believe that in many cases this led to a superficial evangelisation. Let us not forget that many Benedictines were very great missionaries, and their missions were lasting in ways otherwise unknown in Church history. Interestingly, in the Orthodox churches, they maintain a kind of monastic "outreach" especially through the figure of the staretz. My wife tells me that in Transylvania, where members of her family live, almost every town has a staretz. These figures constantly give counsel and spiritual guidance to their people. Sadly, today, I am forced recurrently to counsel fellow Catholics to avoid relationships of "spiritual direction" on account of the dangerous and abusive relationships which Catholic priests routinely seek to establish with vulnerable or dependent faithful, and the ecclesiastical culture of constant movement has led many clerics to think they can get away with such behaviour too.

Of course, as I have argued in other writings, I also think the waning of the temporal power in the Church is a primary cause of this unfortunate clerical culture. That ebbing of the temporal power alongside the clericalization of religious life formed, if you like, the perfect cocktail for the kind of clerical managerialism we have today, which almost exclusively characterises modern Catholic "leadership." The effects of clericalism seem as much a problem among traditionalists as among the rest of the faithful. Some years ago, I delivered a course in philosophy to a group of traditional religious, and it alarmed me that the friars saw their communal religious life and even their vows as little more than just a path by which to become priests. The prophetic character of consecration was remarkably absent from their purview. According to the Orthodox theologian Andrew Louth, the predominant Eastern theological view of monastic life is that monasticism corresponds to the Israelite prophetic ministry in the same way as the Christian priesthood corresponds to the Levitical priesthood. Thus, in the New Covenant, we have two ministries that mirror those of the Old Covenant, but rather than being ordered towards the first coming of the Messiah, they are ordered towards the second coming of Christ in glory as Just Judge. Such a conception of religious life as essentially prophetic rings true and is found scattered throughout official documents of Rome, but practically speaking we Latins have lost sight of its truth and almost nowhere is it lived among us.

Regarding differences between Latin and Greek Christianity, I find Fr Adrian Fortescue a helpful guide. Indeed, I consider Fortescue to have been one of the sanest clerics of his time. I think he was right not only to dive deep into his own liturgical tradition as the architects of revolution were quietly already plotting its destruction, but to take seriously the position of the Eastern Orthodox. I am absolutely sure that the crisis of authority among the Greeks and the crisis of tradition among the Latins will never find their respective solutions until we achieve the reunification of the whole Apostolic Church. In fact, these days I find myself praying for this intention above any other. On this topic, tell me, have you read Geoffrey Hull's *The Banished Heart*? It is amazing to me how little that book is discussed, when it seems to address so many points relevant to us in the Church today.

I read your piece on vocation which you kindly sent to me. Interestingly, I think you and I have a small disagreement on the "naturality of marriage." That is to say, while I agree that—other than by some dramatic equivocation—one cannot have a "calling" to marriage, a baptised member of the Church does not ordinarily enter mere marriage at all, but Holy Matrimony, which is not a natural institution but a sacrament of Christ (even if on being confected it assumes into itself the natural

institution of marriage). And it seems to me that there
is no "calling," properly speaking, to Holy Matrimony *or*
to Holy Orders, as such sacraments are *ordinary* to the
faithful—and therefore it is not necessary to be *called
into them*. Indeed, one might say that such sacraments are
natural to Christians, whose nature has been re-created
and regenerated by the waters of baptism. And hence,
the fact that these sacraments are purely supernatural
does not stop them from being natural *to us*, if indeed
our nature is supernatural by virtue of being supernaturalised by the sacramental life beginning in baptism.

What is *not* merely natural to the sacramental life
of the Christian, but requires a special calling directly
from Christ, is the spousal mystery of religious life,
which is not entered by way of any sacrament, but by
an act of consecration. Hence, it seems to me, when we
speak of what is normative to the Christian life, without
qualification, by "calling" we mean not Holy Matrimony,
not Holy Orders, nor indeed anything else, but religious
consecrated life alone.

I'm very grateful to you for recommending Hannon's
book on St. Thomas's liturgical theology, which I have
now ordered, and I look forward to reading it. I wish
to be clear: I do not accuse Aquinas of bringing about
the cultural shift from understanding the Christian as
a "liturgical person" to a "person who accepts certain
propositions"; nor do I accuse him of entrenching such
a shift in his own works. But I do believe that over
time such a shift happened in the Catholic Church, the
evidence for which I see everywhere, and I deem this
change a theological corruption that has warped our
self-understanding as Christians and downgraded the
primacy of holiness—dare I say, mystical transformation
in Christ—in the lives of the baptised.

I had never before heard of Hilarion Heagy, but I
deeply sympathise with people like that. The Church,
in its human aspect, is eating itself. The Church has

become the great Ouroboros which she was established on earth to replace with the Holy Cross. Those who are scandalised out of the Church will, I am sure, receive some mercy in the end. Since I became a Roman Catholic many years ago, and especially during the seven years I worked as a Church official in the UK, in the institutional Church I have met some of the most corrupt, deranged, and even downright evil people I could ever imagine encountering. Were it not for my conviction that all meaning and purpose in this vale of tears flows directly from the heart of Christ, and that outside the maternal care of His Mother there is only the darkness of the diabolical realm, I would have left the Catholic fold a long time ago. Fortunately, by His grace, I know Him to be the Truth, and so with Him I remain.

It is a great source of sorrow to see how the Church has grown so very alien to herself. One autumnal evening, I attended a lecture in London by a retired Harvard Professor of Hindu Studies. It was in fact a lecture on the Rhineland Mystics. I learned more in that hour, in a talk delivered by a Hindu about the mystical tradition of my own religion, than I had from all the homilies I'd heard over the preceding decade and a half. That is truly a scandal. One sometimes feels that it's only possible to discover authentic Catholicism if one flees the official institution for those corners where people, by virtue of their disassociation with it, are free from the petty power-games and clericalism of the modern Church.

If the hierarchy spent only half the time on disseminating the mystical and liturgical tradition of the Church that it does on destroying our own liturgical inheritance, it could drag us out of the nihilism of the secular age in the flash of a moment. Hence, it surprises me not that people, still longing for a spiritual life and some induction into a living tradition, and seeing that the institutional Church cannot satiate their deepest desires, gravitate towards the works of the perennialists and the modern Sufi scholars. Those people who stumble in the dark and eventually find perennialism and Sufism are themselves orphans, and the Church is the parent that has abandoned them. For this reason, in the decades to come, works of "Catholic perennialists" like Jean Hani, Valentin Tomberg, Jean Borella, Wolfgang Smith, and others will be of the utmost importance for the reevangelisation of the world. Those sophiological writers whom I name have held to the Church understood as a divine and living Being that does not shudder at Her own Mystery.

Forgive me for this long reply. Let us keep each other in prayer. I am forever grateful for your friendship.

Yours in the Lord, as ever,

Sebastian

LETTER 3

Dear Sebastian,

No need to ask forgiveness when you have sent me so many words of wisdom. I am in your debt.

You are certainly quite correct that the ecclesiastical culture of our times is inimical to deep thought, high artistic flights, and ancient symbols. This is why some of the best, most exciting, most promising work is taking place outside the borders of the institution. "Seeds of the Word..."

Regarding the naturalness of the vocation to marriage and clerical life, I still think we may have a disagreement. While priests are natural to the Mystical Body of Christ, the Mystical Body of Christ itself is not natural to mankind, but brought miraculously and surprisingly from God's free gift. So, while man and woman are naturally directed to marry and have children, and this good inclination is blessed, elevated, supernaturally fructified by Christ, I do not think it possible to say that man is naturally directed to a sacramental priesthood centered on offering the unbloody sacrifice of Christ on the Cross. And wherever celibacy is retained as a commitment for priests—I am very much of the belief that this is something Our Lord wishes, contrary to the Eastern Christian view of it—it is clear they are being lifted out of secular life, out of the world of begetting and homesteading, into a sacral realm that is symbolized by the sanctuary of the Church in which (ideally) only they should minister (and in which we allow other men to enter as substitutes for ordained ministers).

I do not know if I'm expressing this argument well. Let me put it this way: the natural priesthood to which man is called belongs to every husband and father in the natural order, but the supernatural priesthood belongs to a supernatural order. In this regard, it has more in common with the religious life, although that is more radical still.

I am fully in agreement with the rest of what you write in your missive.

Geoffrey Hull's *The Banished Heart* is a work of passionate complaint, well-founded, and well-documented. The one reason I hesitate sometimes to recommend it to others is that I feel the author has an exceedingly rosy picture of Eastern Christianity and an exceedingly sour "take" on Western papal history, to the point that the book veers, to my mind, into a polemic that can even become slightly unhinged. (I'm sure plenty of people say that about my own books, come to think of it!) It seems to me that a great strength of Fortescue's *The Orthodox Eastern Church*, to which you alluded in your last letter, is to present a more realistic picture of the strengths and weaknesses of both East and West.[5] Still, that being said, I admit that Hull is a powerful critic of much that richly deserves criticism. You can probably

---

[5] Adrian Fortescue, *The Orthodox Eastern Church* (Lincoln, NE: Os Justi Press, 2024; originally published 1907).

see the influence of Hull on my work, though I rarely cite him.

Speaking of those who feel themselves orphans...look at this communication I received today from a longtime correspondent. It's as if he was reading our minds (LOTH = Paul VI's Liturgy of the Hours):

> I must say, for all the help that the LOTH gives me, every time I try to commit to it more regularly I find myself struck with the fact that it just seems insubstantial. There's just not that much there. It's not substantive or dense. I've considered going over to the Ordinariate's Office, because it is more substantive with the full Psalter (no missing Psalms or verses) and the extended daily Scripture readings (using RSV-2CE and without omissions!). I've used the Monastic Diurnal as well in the past, but I can usually only do two "hours" a day, so one thing I like about the Ordinariate is having the chance to pray through all the Psalms, rather than just the Psalms that are used for Prime and Compline (and, potentially, Sext). Anyway...I just find modern Catholicism so *uncompelling*. And, unfortunately, it seems that the Church just keeps doubling down on its bad decisions. I tend to find people like Jordan Peterson more interesting to listen to than the pope or most bishops. At least when he speaks, it seems like there's something at stake—and he seems to be speaking with honesty and sincerity (even if he's wrong on many things). Almost everything that comes from the Church is warmed over, PC, business-ese.

This is how the most fervent, dedicated, and educated Catholics feel much of the time. If we do not find our way to the heart of the Christian tradition, we will be like castaways, with no home, no rescue, no future. It is such a grace to be awakened to that inexhaustible tradition, whose resources lie all around us, in spite of being neglected by nearly everyone.

Warm regards,
Peter

LETTER 4

Dear Peter,

I am very pleased to continue this exchange with you, by which I am being greatly enriched. Hannon's book, *Thomistic Mystagogy*, arrived today; I look forward to studying its contents.

Your take on Hull's *The Banished Heart* is helpful for me, and I agree that he has an overly romantic view of Eastern Orthodoxy. The real advantage of that book, it seems to me, among other gems therein, is that it shows how Paul VI and the so-called Council "fathers" (more like, "revolutionaries") actively distanced the Catholic Church from the Eastern Orthodox Churches in order to cosy up to Protestants. Hence, they alienated those Christians who actually belonged to the Apostolic Church and were mere dissenters in order to align themselves with outright heretics. Moreover, what Hull demonstrates, quite powerfully in my view, is that the "fathers" undertook this transformation of the Church because they had themselves become largely Protestant in their religion and broader worldview, and they saw Protestants far more as their coreligionists than those who were canonically detached but nonetheless in possession of the full sacramental life. The Catholic Church became, then, practically speaking, just another Protestant sect, and we're all now suffering the consequences of this corruption. When one "zooms out" and views the Vatican II revolution like that, one realises just how apocalyptic the whole situation really is.

I would like to reply to your view of marriage and the naturality of it with regard to human nature. I agree with you that it looks like we might have a real disagreement here, but I will attempt to present my position in even clearer terms so that, if there is indeed a real disagreement as we both suspect, I am at least not misunderstood.

First, I do not claim or suggest that the Mystical Body of Christ is natural to mankind. In that sense, I am in general quite at odds with currents of the *nouvelle théol-ogie*. My position is not that we can collapse nature into supernature, or vice versa. My position is that the Mystical Body of Christ is natural to *baptised* mankind, as the members of baptised humanity are different in their nature from the members of unredeemed man, for they have been quite literally re-created and regenerated by the merits of Christ's sacrifice, made available to them in baptism—by whose waters they were made *new creations*.

I believe, with you, that humans are directed by nature towards marriage, just as I believe humans are directed by their nature towards priestly sacrifice of animal or even human victims (and religious sociology concerning almost every civilisation in history testifies to this reality). Such natural impulses are assumed into the supernatural life of baptised man, and satisfied not by the natural contract of marriage or by the priesthood of natural religion, but by institutions of supernatural origin, namely Holy Matrimony and Holy Orders.

Thus, I do not claim—as I think you think I claim—that man *per se* is naturally ordered towards the priesthood instituted by Christ, but only those members of Christ's Body who receive a special grace so to become priests of the new order of Melchizedek. Put simply, natural man is by nature ordered towards natural priesthood and natural marriage; baptised man is by grace—grace being that which has infused and regenerated his nature—ordered towards supernatural priesthood and supernatural marriage, termed Holy Orders and Holy Matrimony respectively.

Perhaps the difference here is that I do not believe that man, once baptised, has a natural life *and* a supernatural life, as I believe man's whole nature is renewed by grace. Thus, even those things that arise from nature, like eating meals and educating one's children, are assumed into and transformed by grace, and thereby ordered towards different ends than those to which they are ordered when in an unredeemed condition (which, after all, is merely what they are when under the devil's dominion). For example, I do not pray like a Christian but eat like a pagan; rather, every aspect of my life, to the degree I daily convert to life in Christ by the power of His grace, is transformed by Him and ordered towards beatitude.

The fact that man requires a special grace to join and live the Christian ministerial priesthood—just as he would require a special grace to live fully the Christological spousal mystery of Holy Matrimony—should not be conflated with what we mean by "vocation." That he needs special graces to fulfil the purposes of his states of life within the Church should not surprise us given that, being a Christian, it is precisely grace that defines him in any case. Thus, univocally speaking, "vocation" refers to the calling to consecrated religious life alone, also for the reasons I gave in my previous message.

In sum, to put it tritely, and perhaps even in a rather clichéd way, I am not a "two-tier Thomist." My position on the nature-supernature distinction, and the relation of the natural and supernatural virtues, and in turn on the difference between natural and supernatural states of life, is largely in agreement with the position advanced by Andrew Pinsent in *The Second-Person Perspective in Aquinas's Ethics*.[6] Do you know it? I cannot recommend it highly enough.

Forgive me if the case I develop above reads as a little doctrinaire, but I have written this reply to you in haste amid a busy schedule today. In fact, these conversations will undoubtedly be better enjoyed over a bottle of fine Lugana when we meet up on Lake Garda this summer—to which I greatly look forward.

Yours,
Sebastian

---

[6] Andrew Pinsent, *The Second-Person Perspective in Aquinas's Ethics: Virtues and Gifts* (New York: Routledge, 2012).

LETTER 5

Dear Sebastian,

Thank you, as always, for the further thoughts and precisions.

Your position has the advantage of making good sense out of the quite traditional grouping of the sacraments of marriage and holy orders as "sacraments for (or having to do with) the good of the community," as distinguished from sacraments that perfect the individual by ingrafting him into Christ: baptism, confirmation, Eucharist (the sacraments of initiation, the last being also the sacrament of perfection in charity), penance, and anointing. All of these pertain to the individual within the Mystical Body, whereas marriage pertains to a baptized man and a baptized woman who come together precisely as the nucleus of a domestic church, a social entity, a community or multiplicity. Similarly, a man is made a minister, or a priest or bishop, for the good of others (*servus servorum Dei*). Even a hermit priest is offering sacrifice "for his own sins and the sins of others," as we read about in the Epistle to the Hebrews (he's doing plenty more than that, but you understand my point). The minister's vocation is essentially a social one.

The consecrated life, in contrast, has nearly always been understood as the perfect living out of the baptismal vocation. Thus, while religious nearly always live in community, and communal life is vitally important to their practice of virtue and their liturgical prayer, nevertheless the state in life as such is a perfection of the individual. It is a sort of "super-baptism" in which one's entire life is turned into a liturgical offering, an embracing of God and renunciation of the evil one as we promise in baptism. Everyone is supposed to do that, but the religious expressly and totally commits himself or herself to the task of living the life of the world to come even now. This is not even possible, practically,

for the married, and it is not easily compatible with
the duties of the parochial priesthood. Again, as Louis
Bouyer so finely expounds in his book on monasticism,
there is no dualism here: the laity and clergy look to the
religious as their lighthouse or exemplar, as the religious
look to the virginal Christ and His virginal Mother as
their exemplars. All are bound into one, in spite of the
often very great differences in their ways of life.

You can argue on behalf of your view that as the
husband and wife are drawn sacramentally into the
relationship of Christ and the Church (cf. Eph 5), so
too the priest is drawn sacramentally into the supreme
priesthood of Christ, that he may offer gifts and sacrifices in and with Christ, for His Body. I will admit
that, seen this way, there is much more of an analogy
than a disanalogy. On the other hand, and this is my
point, man and wife are not "chosen out of" humanity
in order to live the married life, for this is indeed what
they were created for, it belongs to the original order
of creation. Of course Christ the Lord will elevate it,
as He elevates all things. Whereas with a priest of the
Old Law or, even more, of the New Law, he is "chosen
out of" men to be appointed as a priest, as again the
Epistle to the Hebrews explains so well; and the divine
offering he is empowered to offer is not something that
belonged to the order of nature, but is entirely given
from above. That is, the "natural priesthood" of offering
various things to the gods stands at a further distance
from the "supernatural priesthood" that offers either
Christ or signs of Christ than "natural marriage" stands
from "sacramentalized marriage."

While I respect all the Christian anthropologists who
would like to "read back into" pagan sacrifices their like-
nesses to the one true sacrifice, I think these parallels
are at best analogies, at times almost tragic simulacra,
since the rather desperate efforts of pagans to placate
their vengeful gods cannot really be considered true

worship by any stretch of the imagination. According to St. Augustine, indeed, most of the time they were placating demons who tried to lead them away from God. Whereas one need not "read into" natural marriage its likeness to sacramental marriage, since sacramental marriage is nothing other than natural marriage divinely lived by grace, the order of creation subsumed into and transfigured by the order of redemption. There is a direct line connecting an unbaptised man's marrying an unbaptised woman for love and for children to a Christian man's marrying a Christian woman so as to enter into the perfect union of charity and fecundity of Christ and His Church. I simply do not see that such a direct line can be drawn from what you are calling natural priesthood to supernatural priesthood.

Coming around finally to your provocative remark about "two-tier Thomism," this is an extremely subtle question, as you know; for we want something like a Chalcedonian "united but not confused, distinct but not divided." The tendency of the *nouvelle théologie* has been to conflate these domains. There was, recently, a very interesting exchange between Bishop Robert Barron and D. C. Schindler in which they say that their resistance to Catholic political integralism is based on the fact that it distinguishes between the natural and supernatural orders—a distinction with which they as Balthasarians are uncomfortable. Schindler gives the game away at the very end of their exchange when he says, "It seems to me that if the Church's claim is true it has to be the case that...what the Church is proposing is in fact, at the very depths, what everybody actually believes and wants," to which Barron responds: "and I hold that." There it is. Everybody already has faith simply in virtue of being human: "a blind sentiment of religion welling up from the depths of the subconscious under the impulse of the heart and the motion of a will trained to morality," as St. Pius X put it in his encyclical *Pascendi* against the Modernists.

This conflation of natural religion with supernatural transformation, I submit, radically undermines the source of Christian salvation as the free initiative of God taking pity on our fallen nature and intervening with revelation and the grace of faith, with all that comes in its train. Yes, that revelation encounters something in us that welcomes it and recognizes it, but it is still a surprise, an intervention, a miracle, a wonder that utterly transcends all that our reason and nature contain, or lay claim to, or envision. This, again, is where I see a great difference between holy matrimony and holy orders: Christian matrimony is not something that utterly transcends in that way, and it seems to me possible to envision it vaguely and hopefully, as if reaching out toward a perfection already adumbrated; whereas the priesthood of Christ is something introduced into the world by the omnipotent fiat of a God who, in His radical, foolish, self-emptying love for mankind, descends in the womb of the Virgin and becomes man.

Warm regards,
Peter

LETTER 6

Dear Peter,

Thank you for your reply. Much of what you write I am wholly in agreement with, and in some ways your reply appears to argue the case I am trying to develop in this dialogue. I shall therefore only address those parts of your response on which I think there is some difference of opinion, either because we hold different positions or because we hold similar positions but emphasise different aspects of those positions.

First, I agree with you that religious life is given to the Church as the perfection of the sacramental life which begins in baptism. But I would say that it cannot *only* be the perfection of baptism, or reducible to this facet.

That it is so irreducible, it seems to me, is indicated by the traditional practice of receiving a new name at the moment of consecration. As you know, from a biblical perspective, a new name implies a new mission. If consecration only entailed the perfection of the mission given to us all in baptism, receiving a new name would not make sense. Indeed, I believe that Vatican II's *Perfectae Caritatis* got it wrong to suggest that religious might cease to take new names on consecration, which the document pressed in order to emphasise their baptismal mission. Religious life, I would submit, entails a calling into a special spousal state with Jesus Christ which is not normative to the baptised, but is extraordinary, and requires a vocation univocally speaking.

Second, I would wish to contest your view that "Christ the Lord elevates natural marriage as He elevates all things," for not all things are elevated to the level of a sacrament. The fact that Holy Matrimony is a *sacrament*, and has not merely been elevated as a natural good for supernatural ends, in the same way as our ability to sing or create art has been *elevated*—but rather, Holy Matrimony has been *instituted* directly by Christ—should indicate to us that it shouldn't be grouped together with those things that have merely been "elevated." Just as a priest is an icon of Christ the Priest, who is the only Priest, and in whose Priesthood all ministerial priests merely participate, so too a couple assumed into Holy Matrimony are an icon of Christ's union with His Church. No natural marriage can be such an icon, for the reason that no natural marriage—however good—can be a conduit of sanctifying grace, and it is for the sake of flooding mankind with sanctifying grace that Christ is wedded to the Church, a union He consummated on Calvary. Hence, I do not see Holy Matrimony as "nothing other than natural marriage divinely lived by grace," as you put it, just as I do not see the Christian priesthood as nothing other than natural priesthood divinely lived by grace (as you seemed to think I was arguing). Rather, I see both Holy Matrimony and Holy Orders as new institutions established directly by Jesus Christ, fitting for a new creation called *baptised man*.

Third, allow me to clarify what I meant by my "provocative" comment regarding "two-tier Thomism." I do not accept that baptised man's natural virtues remain in and of themselves unchanged other than by being subordinated to supernatural virtues received from without, as for example is seemingly argued occasionally by John of St. Thomas, who at times exhibits a liking for both mechanical and vertical metaphors that are not to be found in the writings of Aquinas (indeed, on more than one occasion Garrigou-Lagrange misattributes to Aquinas metaphors—especially for the gifts and fruits of the Holy Ghost—invented by John of St. Thomas). In short, I do not think we have nature intact, with supernature plopped on top. I believe that supernature regenerates our whole nature, and thus natural prudence, for example, is infused with, and transformed by, supernatural prudence, leaving our natural virtue of prudence transfigured by its supernatural counterpart given to us by grace. This, I hold, is Aquinas's true teaching, which we see when we free ourselves from modern paradigms and stop reading quantity-heavy metaphors into his texts (which he himself does not opt for). Nor, though, do I accept the view of von Balthasar et al. that the supernatural life merely renders explicit our natural capacity for union with God. This, I hold, is a fundamental misunderstanding of traditional theology's conception of what is meant by "connaturality." Just because supernature does not do violence to our nature, that does not mean it merely illumines what is already possessed by nature. Indeed, interestingly enough, the anthropology of the *nouvelle théologie*'s key figures corresponds to how Aquinas sees the fall of Satan: Aquinas says that Satan rebelled when he discovered that he would have to receive the beatific vision by grace rather than as a capacity of his angelic nature.[7] In turn, what those modern theologians argue for *their* nature corresponds exactly to what Satan argued for his nature.

Unfortunately, Catholic theology has tended to oscillate between a vertical—Cartesian-influenced—two-tier Thomism that in its worst exhibitions presents the Christian as a kind of moral schizophrenic, and a collapsing of supernature into nature in a way that naturalises the whole Christian Mystery. I reject both positions. For a while, I thought the way to escape this dichotomy was that of rejecting the Thomist account of grace as "created supernature" in favour of the Palamite conception of grace as uncreated divine *energeia* (which after all has never been condemned by Rome, and might seem to better explain the experience of many of Latin Christianity's great mystics, e.g., John of the Cross, Meister Eckhart, Nicholas of Cusa, and others). But it was reading Andrew Pinsent's book *The Second-Person Perspective in Aquinas's Ethics*, mentioned in a previous missive to you, that convinced me not only of the veracity of St. Thomas's account of grace, but also that his position has been widely misunderstood, and repeatedly so, which is in large part the reason for Catholic theology's unfortunate proclivity to oscillate between two errors and rarely to land on the truth, the practical living of which has routinely been nothing short of disastrous. Thus, I argue neither for the naturalist account of supernature (perpetuated—as you observe—by Barron and Schindler), nor the mechanical pseudo-Thomism that has so often plagued the low-grade manuals of Catholic seminaries. At the risk of appearing conceited, I claim to stick with St. Thomas.

Yours in the Lord, as ever,
Sebastian

---

[7] See *Summa Theologiae* I, Q. 63, art. 3.

LETTER 7

Dear Sebastian,

I have thought for a long time—and I'm sure this idea has already been worked out in detail by other theologians—that the hypostatic union of the Incarnate Word offers us a template for understanding analogously what is true of the union of nature and grace. That is, the infusion and influence of grace must be to the depths of the person, so that we are not looking at a Nestorian "two persons" scenario: the man Jesus of Nazareth and the Son of God, as if in us there is the natural man with all his natural capacities, and then a supernatural something-or-other that rides on top, making use of nature but not entering into and transforming it, rather like a rider on his horse: a fine collaboration but no more than that. Instead, grace must be, to use the wonderful phrase of older spiritual writers, the life of my soul, as my soul is the life of my body. What makes the body alive is the soul, entirely present in every part of it; and what makes the soul alive is sanctifying grace, bringing every power of the soul to *deiformitas* or conformity to God, and empowering it for supernatural action. So, indeed, not a two-tiered system but a unified vision of human-divine flourishing, analogous (again) to the theandric activity of Christ.

On the other hand, there is an almost monophysite fusion of nature and grace on the part of the de Lubacians and the Rahnerians, albeit in contrary ways, as Fr Serafino Lanzetta nicely explains in his little book *God's Abode with Man: The Mystery of Divine Grace.*[8] Again, the ancient formula "united but not confused, distinct but not divided" comes to mind.

As for the rest of what you've written, it has given me much to ponder. Thank you again for taking the

---

[8] Serafino Lanzetta, *God's Abode with Man: The Mystery of Divine Grace* (Lincoln, NE: Os Justi Press, 2023).

time to work out your position so convincingly. I look forward to future exchanges prompted by our common passion for the truth in Jesus Christ.

Yours in Him,
Peter

APPENDIX 2
A Response to Rod Dreher's *Living in Wonder*

WHEN the manuscript of the book you hold in your hands was being compiled, the popular conservative writer Rod Dreher sent me the manuscript of his own book, entitled *Living in Wonder: Finding Mystery and Meaning in a Secular Age*, which at the time was not to be published for another five months.[1] Given that his book seemed to address many of the themes which my own book sought to engage, I read Dreher's manuscript with great interest.

Dreher has an uncanny ability to identify the topic around which conversation among conservative-minded people is going to orbit for the coming years, and then write the primer on it, thereby both framing and shaping that conversation for at least the ensuing decade. It is frankly astonishing. I don't know how he does it, but he does it repeatedly. Back-to-the-land, weightlifting, organic-farmsteading, home-schooling conservatives are widely referred to as "crunchy cons" to this day.[2] "Benedict Option" has entered the conservative lexicon and now you only need to throw the phrase into a discussion about society for everyone immediately to know both the diagnosis and solutions to which you're referring. Since the publication of his book *Live Not By Lies*, it has become a staple of conservative discourse to identify our current progressivist politics as Marxist in form, content, and operation, and it is common to claim that Christians need to learn from those who survived Soviet regimes.[3] At each stage of

---

[1] *Living in Wonder: Finding Mystery and Meaning in a Secular Age* (Grand Rapids, MI: Zondervan, 2024).
[2] *Crunchy Cons* (New York: Crown, 2006).
[3] *Live Not By Lies: A Manual For Dissidents in Christian Countries* (London: Hodder & Stoughton, 2024; originally published in 2020).

the development of the conservative discussion, Dreher writes the must-have book.

Well, he's done it again. *Living in Wonder* is a book about "re-enchantment," a word that one currently hears on almost every conservative podcast and reads in almost every conservative Substack post. The materialist, pro-gressivist, efficiency-based paradigm in which we've been entrenched for decades—centuries, even—is spiralling into oblivion as we have realised that we can neither live without meaning nor author meaning out of our own personal post-modern journeys of self-discovery.

If the choice is between living in a meaning-vacuum and death, we will choose death. Meaninglessness is why suicide is the number one cause of death in the West among teenagers and young adults. At a macro level, this choice for death is seen in the decision of entire nations to stop inducting the few remaining children they have into their cultural and civilisational inher-itance, while preventing further children by recourse to contraception- and abortion-technologies. In short, we cannot stand a life without meaning, and since we don't know how to recover meaning, we've decided to annihilate ourselves.

Dreher, however, thinks that we *can* recover meaning and purpose in our lives. *Living in Wonder* is his guide to this great recovery and an invitation to be part of it. The key, he tells us, is that of re-enchanting our world...but what exactly does *he* mean by this? Dreher seems largely to mean what I mean, namely that we must rediscover the ancient Neoplatonic participation-emanation ontology of the pre-modern mind, though he does not put it quite like that. In Dreher's words:

> In the medieval model, everything in the visible and invisible world was connected through God. All things had ultimate meaning because they par-ticipated in the life of the Creator. The specifics of that participatory relationship were matters of

dispute among theologians, but few if any doubted
that this was how the cosmos worked.[4]

Later in the book, Dreher is more explicit about the
primacy of this participation-emanation metaphysics
for the recovery of an enchanted worldview. Indeed, he
emphasises what Thomists—philosophers whom Dreher
regrettably attacks throughout his volume, grouping
them together with Calvinists[5]—call the "exemplarism
of the divine mind":

> Humans participate in the life of God through the
> logoi—the essential reasons for being—embedded
> within ourselves and all created things. The logoi
> within creation are in a real sense the incarna-
> tion of God's ideas. Our divinely ordained task as
> humans is to elevate all things to deeper partic-
> ipation in the Logos.... Contemplating created
> things—stars, mountains, paintings, violin quartets,
> or the intricate form of a child's ear—is in a real
> sense to contemplate God through the visible or
> audible signs of his handiwork.[6]

In other words, the world is God's Icon. For Dreher,
then, the fundamental prerequisite for re-enchanting
our world is that of relinquishing the "dead matter"
cosmology which modernity has handed us. Then we
can return to a theocentric conception of the universe
and how it is always held in being by God, Whom it
in turn reflects. Once the world is seen as participating *in* God insofar as it exists and emanating *from* His
divine mind insofar as it is intelligible, Dreher thinks
we're only a short step away from seeing the world's
history—including our own personal histories—under
the aspect of providentialism.

Moreover, Dreher says, this enchanted vision of our
world and ourselves entails the normativity of miracles,
angelic agency, and ultimately a meaning-filled life, to all

---

[4] Dreher, *Living in Wonder*, 17.
[5] Dreher, 78.
[6] Dreher, 200.

of which we've grown blind on account of the modern mechanistic paradigm. Ultimately, then, "enchanted" is simply the term Dreher uses to refer to "the widespread belief that, in the words of an Orthodox prayer, God is everywhere present and fills all things."[7]

"For many Christians in this present time," Dreher writes, "the vivid sense of spiritual reality that our enchanted ancestors had has been drained of its life force."[8] He is not so naïve, however, as to think that the acceptance of Christian propositions or vague respect for Christianity as a possible "ethical code" will suffice to address the so-called "meaning crisis." Many—perhaps most—Christians are just as under the spell of modernity as everyone else, having allowed modernity's prejudices and assumptions to colonise their minds, willingly or not. For this reason, Dreher doesn't only masterfully weave into his case an array of highly illustrative and informative (and entertaining!) anecdotes—from demon-possessed housewives to Chestertonian Italians—but he engages in a very interesting application of Iain McGilchrist's neuroscientific work on the hemispheric relations of the human brain, suggesting that re-enchantment will require a better formation of right-brain thinking.[9]

Having accepted the overly rationalistic, reductionist mentality of modernity, we tend to think that Christianity is solely about a contractual agreement with a "Lord and Saviour" in exchange for which we are handed eternal life, or that it's a mere intellectual assent to doctrinal propositions, or that it's a helpful moral framework. Basically, the mystery and the wonder are gone. Worship and miracles—that is, I-You encounter with God through the transformative mystery of His love—has become little more than Christianity's window dressing.

---

[7] Dreher, 17.
[8] Dreher, 19.
[9] See Iain McGilchrist, *The Master and His Emissary: The Divided Brain and the Making of the Western World* (New Haven, CT: Yale University Press, 2010), 133–208.

Dreher thinks we've got it the wrong way round, and that's perhaps unsurprising, given that he's now a practising Orthodox Christian, and mystery and wonder are two things the Orthodox do *very* well. "I am convinced that the only way to revive the Christian faith," Dreher asserts, "which is fading fast from the modern world, is not through moral exhortation, legalistic browbeating, or more effective apologetics but through mystery and the encounter with wonder."[10]

Dreher's analysis is far from narrow, nor is it solely esoteric. For example, he takes seriously the spiritually crushing consequences of modernist aesthetics and what this has meant with regard to architecture and the built environment:

> It is sometimes said that you can tell what is most important to a society by which buildings are its tallest. In the medieval era, the spires of cathedrals towered over the cities of the West. Today, skyscrapers of banks and corporations stand like giants watching over our metropolises. Our buildings tell the true tale of who and what we worship.[11]

Now, in the cities of our world—which are no longer consoling settlements of human assembly and culture, but polluted, bustling hives—populations are dominated by temples to mammon. Our built environment teaches us that material wealth, and hence the escalation of production and consumption, are all the world is for.

The base materialism of the West in particular—though this is a moral corruption that we have successfully spread around the rest of the world—is a direct consequence, Dreher notes, of the disappearance of meaning (or, as certain Christian phenomenologists would have it, "value") from our world. "If nothing has intrinsic sacramental value," writes Dreher, "then the best way to measure the value of things is by putting a price tag on

---

[10] Dreher, *Living in Wonder*, 27.
[11] Dreher, 45.

them."[12] And it was only a matter of time, he says, before we applied this view of the world—and how the only meaning the world can possess is that which it derives from the market—to our very own bodies. The sexual revolution and all the unhappiness that has come with it, then, is inseparable from the desecrating process of bleeding the world dry of intrinsic meaning and purpose.

Many people have long intuited that we are in a "meaning crisis" and one of the seductive ways that we have attempted to escape it is through the internet and the growing social media platforms now available to us. But "the internet can be thought of as a vast disenchantment machine," Dreher says, and cannot deliver that for which we look to it.[13] There is a simple reason why the internet is so dangerous according to Dreher: it "destroys our ability to focus attention."[14] Poor attention among modern people is a catastrophe, Dreher thinks, because the theocentric, participation-emanation view of the cosmos is only recovered by way of the ability to attend to it and thus really *see* reality.

Dreher is in good company. As already noted in this volume, the eighteenth-century Jesuit priest Jean Pierre de Caussade insisted that deep spiritual insight came through practising attention to the "sacrament of the present moment." The renowned French philosopher Simone Weil wrote a great deal about *union with reality* requiring a deep and habituated practice of attention.[15] Valentin Tomberg taught that "attention without effort" was the vital practice needed to overcome the "hex" that modernity has placed on our minds, and thereby see the world as meaningful and infused with the divine presence.[16]

---

[12] Dreher, 46.
[13] Dreher, 47.
[14] Dreher, 49.
[15] See the recent fascinating study of this topic—with a special focus on Weil—by Silvia Caprioglio Panizza, entitled *The Ethics of Attention: Engaging the Real with Iris Murdoch and Simone Weil* (New York: Routledge, 2022).
[16] See Tomberg, *Meditations*, 3–26.

Dreher tells us that "attention—what we pay attention to, and how we attend—is the most important part of the mindset needed for re-enchantment."[17] Having broken our ability to attend to reality in all its splendour, in favour of virtual reality, the internet has locked us up within ourselves—*selves* which we then try to re-create in numerous phantoms through online avatars. The "virtual self" of the internet age is modernity's realisation of its anthropology.

The internet has allowed us fully to adopt an anthropological dualism that separates *self* and *body* as if this conception of human nature were not a controversial hypothesis requiring demonstration but a truth to be assumed. Now, through technology, we are seeking to make the fiction of Descartes' "self"—that is, the ghostly *res cogitans* encaged in the fleshly prison of the *res extensa*—an existential reality:

> What the modern gnostics have done—most shockingly in the rise of gender ideology, which denies that the body has anything to do with one's sex—is to separate humanity radically from the material world. To these true believers, the self is defined entirely by the mind; the body is irrelevant. The next step beyond transgenderism is transhumanism, which means the assimilation of the human into the wholly controllable realm of technology.[18]

For Dreher the trouble is this: the isolated, atomised, autonomous "self" that modern man considers himself to be simply cannot discover the enchanted world, however much he might desire to do so. Dreher offers the example of the English writer Katherine May, who has written a book entitled *Enchantment*.[19] In that book, May bemoans the fact that she has no rituals in her life, and no one to tell her how to get any and perform them. She says that

---

[17] Dreher, *Living in Wonder*, 158.
[18] Dreher, 50.
[19] Katherine May, *Enchantment: Awakening Wonder in an Anxious Age* (New York: Riverhead Books, 2023).

she would like to join a congregation of worshippers—not necessarily Christian—who will tolerate her turning up unreliably and never fully getting involved. Basically, she wants a community that will allow her to privilege her "individuality" and "autonomy" above everything, even amid shared, collective religiosity. But that is precisely the problem. Either you see yourself as reality's author at the centre of everything and thereby land yourself in a meaningless world, or you surrender yourself to something bigger than you in an act of self-renunciation—of *kenosis*, to use the theological term of art—by virtue of which your life can be flooded with meaning and purpose.

For Dreher, if we are going to rediscover the world as enchanted—that is, as participating in the life of God, Who is in turn intimately bound up with it everywhere and at all times—we must begin to see the world as it really is. This means turning away from the hall of mirrors that *is* the modern, insulated self. According to Dreher, freedom from the prison of the self, to enter enchanted reality, not only requires attentive observation of the world in all its marvellous particularity and majesty, but *participatory* experience of the world. As he puts it:

> Re-enchantment is not about imposing fanciful nostalgia onto the world, like coating a plain yellow cake with pastel fondant frosting. Instead, it is about learning how to perceive what already exists and reestablishing participatory contact with the really real. God has already enchanted the world; it is up to us to clear away the scales from our eyes, recognize what is there, and establish a relationship with it.[20]

Hence, Dreher not only highlights the work of McGilchrist in the area of participatory perception but also turns to an analysis first posited by the Hungarian-American psychologist Mihaly Csikszentmihalyi concerning the "flow state," also mentioned earlier in this volume. According

---

[20] Dreher, *Living in Wonder*, 55.

to Csikszentmihalyi, entering what he called the "flow state" allows people to suspend the abstractionist tendencies of the mind—especially the modern mind—and attend to the real *in union with it*. People experience such states while rock climbing, practising martial arts, dancing, training with a steel mace, and so forth.[21]

"Flow" has gained renewed interest in recent years due to the creative and original work on this subject by John Vervaeke. The lack of flow in modern life is associated among psychologists with a rise in depression and other emotional disorders. And as previously noted, there is also a growing industry of *counterfeit flow*, found in social media and computer games that offer the opportunities for all the acute attention without any of the embodiment needed for genuine flow and its positive effects. Until we learn to flow again, Dreher insists, we will not learn to wonder at reality.

For Dreher, more than propositional religion, the soul needs existential nourishment. We are nourished by attending to reality, both by being interiorly present to it and by developing ways by which to enter the flow state. Such a change from sightlessness to the enchanted vision, however, requires liberation from what McGilchrist and others have called the "monkey brain"—the constantly chattering, obsessive, distracting mentality that torments us and ever prevents us from enjoying interior peace. Dreher explains that in this regard he was greatly helped by an ancient practice, traceable back to the first Christian monastics of the Egyptian desert, called the "Jesus Prayer." Using a knotted "prayer rope," on the advice of his Orthodox pastor Dreher spent an hour everyday meditating on a short supplicatory prayer uttered on each knot as the rope

---

[21] See chapter 12 above. I have written elsewhere about how I've enjoyed intense switches into "flow" whilst hunting. See my essay entitled "The Theurgy of Deer Stalking," *The European Conservative*, May 14, 2024, https://europeanconservative.com/articles/essay/the-theurgy-of-deer-stalking/.

passed through his hand. Eventually, he says, his mind was quieted and his soul was ordered towards adoration.

Once we see the world as it really is, that doesn't mean that behind the veil of modernity's "dead matter" conception of reality there is a cosy, fluffy Disneyland. In fact, in the enchanted world—the world as it really is—we have to contend with all sorts of evil forces, including innumerable demons who want to destroy us. And as Dreher wanders into an analysis of the darker side of the enchanted world, things get very strange in the book.

When, in chapter 6 of *Living in Wonder*, Dreher began to discuss UFOs as evil "gods" who have been visiting our planet, with which globalists and technocrats have long been communicating, I was poised to dismiss it as too much crackpottery. But if you think the world really *is* full of meaning, and that you can learn a lot more about how things really are from the great religious wisdom traditions than from our modern reductionism, why wouldn't you consider the unfolding events of recent history in the light of such traditions? And as it happens, every great religious wisdom tradition in the world, including Christianity, holds that the cosmos is full of evil spirits who like to interfere with our lives.

The erudite writer Paul Kingsnorth, who has considerably influenced Dreher, has claimed that modern technologies are opening the world up to enslavement by occult powers of a demonic nature. In Kingsnorth's view, we are all insufficiently aware of what is happening to us. He doesn't claim to understand it all completely, but he's quite sure that modern technologies, especially fast-developing AI technologies, are channels for the evil spirits which man has otherwise been attempting to withstand or appease since time immemorial.

Religiosity the world over has sought to keep the evil spirits away or at least curtail their wrath, but perhaps we're now letting them into our homes and even into our trouser pockets through "smart technology" (whose talismanic logo, many have noted, is the symbol of man's fall to Satan's temptation). And by way of such technology, those evil spirits may be taking possession of our minds. That, at least, is where Dreher speculates all this is going. For him, digital culture is the earthly realisation of the sphere in which malignant spirits reside, and hence by this culture the ancient "gods—Baal, Ishtar, and Moloch—have returned and are asserting their dark power over the post-Christian world."[22]

In Dreher's view, the grave imperative facing modern man, especially if we're to subdue the demonic and technologically-driven takeover of our world, is that of embracing the mystical life and entering intimate union with God. Only by a theocentric—and therefore *true*—mysticism will man be able to contend with the dark mysticism, the "occult power," that Dreher thinks is rapidly gaining ground. And it is to the theme of recentring modern man's struggle on the rediscovery of mysticism that Dreher devotes the final chapter of his book.

Having read the book now in your hands, you will imagine the depth of my sympathy with Dreher's case in *Living in Wonder*. His book is a significant achievement and a gripping read. It is filled with fascinating studies of important thinkers and creative applications of their research; with marvellous anecdotes, some of which are deeply personal; and it achieves an impressive breadth without falling into shallowness over the complex topics with which it engages. Nonetheless, I was left with qualms, which I will explore below.

I have insisted throughout this volume that the question of the nature-supernature relation (or the nature-grace distinction, if you like) that has traditionally preoccupied theologians is absolutely essential to a Christian account of re-enchantment. Indeed, in this present book, the nature-supernature relation has been at the heart of

---

[22] Dreher, *Living in Wonder*, 155.

the case I have developed. If we don't get our account
of this topic right, in our quest to re-enchant our world
we will oscillate between a view of nature that under-
estimates its fallenness and a mysticism that has little
to do with our embodied existence in the world—two
errors to be avoided.

As it happens, all ecclesial communities are stuck in a
rut over this issue. Catholics have tended to posit three
categories: 1) *uncreated supernature*, i.e., God; 2) *created
nature*, i.e., everything God has made; and 3) *created
supernature*, i.e., grace, by which God shares His divine
life with what He has made. Inaccurate presentations of
this tripartite account have repeatedly led Catholics to
view creation as a two-tier system, with grace plopped
by God on top of nature. The practical upshot of such
a misunderstanding has recurrently been unendurable
spiritual and moral schizophrenia among Catholics, with
weird "vertical metaphors" applied to the interrelation
between the so-called natural and supernatural virtues.
Moreover, it has led to an insufferable quasi-Gnostic
clericalism which sees nature—baptised or otherwise—as
"secular" in the modern sense, with the priestly hierarchy implicitly deemed a kind of *"perfecti"* on account of
its offices being purely of supernatural origin. In turn,
"Church" has gradually come to be erroneously identified
with "priesthood" rather than "all the Faithful."

Seeking to escape this theological pathology, Catholic
modernists, rather than offering a truer account of the
nature-supernature relation, simply collapsed supernature into nature. This strategic error allowed for the
destruction of Catholic orthodoxy and orthopraxis in the
mid-twentieth century, from which the Catholic Church
has not yet recovered. (Protestant reformers identified
this problem in Catholic theology centuries ago and
thought they could evade it by altogether rejecting one
of the categories as a source of God's revelation, namely
created nature, and they thus paved the way to the "dead

matter" cosmology that undergirds those aspects of modernity which Dreher rightly criticises.)

The Eastern Orthodox have come to posit two categories: 1) *uncreated supernature*, i.e., God, and 2) *created nature*, i.e., everything God has made. Prominent theologians like Gregory Palamas in the fourteenth century unsystematically argued that God's "divine energies" are extended to nature from His essence, and that's really all we mean by "grace." Since, though, His energies and His essence are not *really*—but only *conceptually*—distinct (otherwise God's simplicity and indivisibility would be undermined), Catholic theologians have wondered how such a view does not lead to a kind of hidden pantheism of the Spinozan kind. Ultimately, the Catholic concern is that the Orthodox account entails reducing Christianity to a species of natural religion. With regard to practice, some claim that the Orthodox view may not be unrelated to the unfortunate tendency among its adherents to divinise temporal powers and stray into excessive nationalism, which down the ages has been called the error of "caesaropapism."

As such, what Dreher says, namely that "after the triumph of Christianity and the vanquishing of Greco-Roman paganism, Christians did not make a sharp distinction between the natural and the supernatural," and that only much later "the Latin Church began to separate 'nature' and 'supernature,'" is simply untrue.[23] The nature-supernature relation has always been at the heart of Christian theology, even if theologians of different traditions have disagreed over what is the correct understanding of the relation. And as Prof. Marcus Plested has irrefutably demonstrated in his extensive scholarship on the topic, prior to the fall of Constantinople to Muslim invaders, Thomas Aquinas's account of the nature-supernature relation was the one accepted

---

[23] Dreher, 37, 38.

by many—perhaps the majority—of the Orthodox theologians in the Greek world and beyond.[24]

Due to, in my view, Dreher's insufficient engagement
with the nature-supernature relation, he makes certain
claims that appear to me irreconcilable with a Christian
case for re-enchantment. That case, it seems to me, must
fully acknowledge the fallenness of this sinful world (and
hence its need for a Saviour) and avoid flirting with the
nature-worship of paganism. For example, early in his
book, Dreher claims that Christian sacerdotal blessing
offers nothing new to the world which it doesn't already
have: "when a priest blesses water, turning it into holy
water, he is not adding something to it to change it; he
is rather making the water more fully what it already is:
a carrier of God's grace."[25] In contrast to such a view,
Tomberg wrote the following:

> The world is not what it should be. There is a
> contradiction between the totality and the details.
> For whilst the starry heavens represent a harmony
> of equilibrium and perfect cooperation, animals
> and insects devour one another and innumerable
> legions of infectious microbes bear sickness and
> death to men, animals and plants. It is this con-
> tradiction which the term "the Fall" alludes to. In
> the first place, it designates a state of affairs in the
> world which gives the impression that the world
> is composed of two independent, if not opposed,
> worlds, as if in the organism of the great world
> of the "harmony of the spheres" there is interpo-
> lated another world with its own laws and evolu-
> tion—as if a cancerous outgrowth has taken place
> in the otherwise healthy organism of the great
> world.... The ancients always knew that there
> is an anomaly in the state of the world. Whether
> they attributed it to the principle of ignorance
> ("*avidya*") as in ancient India, or to the principle
> of darkness (Ahriman) as in ancient Persia, or

---

[24] See Marcus Plested, *Orthodox Readings of Aquinas* (Oxford: Oxford
University Press, 2012).
[25] Dreher, *Living in Wonder*, 20.

again to the principle of evil (Satan) as the ancient
Semites did, is not important; it is always a matter of distinction between the natural world and
the unnatural world, between the natural and the
perverse, between health and sickness.[26]

As Tomberg notes, the world is sick and inescapably
trapped in a cycle of rebellion and violence. In its total-
ity the world conveys something of the majesty and
beauty of its Author, and yet on inspection we find that
it's ridden with defacements and corruptions of every
kind. This is why the world is no longer in and of itself
a bearer of grace, and is described rather as "fallen."
Moreover, that is why grace must enter the world from
without in order to redeem it from within, the effect of
which is twofold: healing and elevation.

Dreher insists that Christian re-enchantment requires
a rejection of "the world of neo-paganism and the occult,"
which he says has now been "opened wide."[27] But due
to his lack of engagement with the nature-supernature
relation, there are curious passages in the book in which
he seems to present Christianity as little more than a
species of natural religion, and thus a kind of paganism—even if a paganism of which he would approve.

"All Christians of the first 1,300 years of the faith," he
tells us, "shared with the pagans this sacramental vision:
a material world saturated with spiritual meaning and
power."[28] But they *didn't* share it. Christians understood
the world as saturated with spiritual meaning because
they saw it to unfold out of the Godhead in its awe-
inspiring intelligibility and to be filled with angels and
saints who interact with us. The pagan "sacramental
vision" saw the world as a realm of mischievous gods
who torment us and who must be appeased at all times
with violent sacrifices and the prizes of war. What the

---

[26] Tomberg, *Meditations*, 245–46.
[27] Dreher, *Living in Wonder*, 100.
[28] Dreher, 33.

pagans worshipped as gods the Christians derided as demons. Moreover, when Dreher comes to tell us why Christianity won out over the pagan religions, we discover that it was because the former was superior to the latter by degree, not different in kind: "the 'magic' of the Christians was more powerful than the magic of the pagan priests and sorcerers."[29]

Intermittently, albeit inadvertently, conflating Christianity and paganism amid a sustained attack on the latter was confusing as I read Dreher's book, especially as he urgently tells us that "people today aren't wrong to seek enchantment—but if they do it outside a clearly and uniquely Christian path, they will inevitably be drawn into the demonic."[30] So...which is it? Are Christians mere supercharged pagans, sharing with all pagans the same "sacramental vision," only a better version of it, or do they reject the world of paganism as demonic? I was left guessing as to what Dreher thought.

With that said, Dreher is very clear about one thing: "Enchantment—the restoration of flow among God, the natural world, and us—begins with desiring God, and all his manifestations, or theophanies, in our lives."[31] That, most certainly, is the central message of the book, and one that our world desperately needs to hear if we're to escape the paradigm of modernity that has painted the whole world grey and severed us from any apprehension of God, Who in reality is, as St. Augustine said, closer to us than we are to ourselves: "interior intimo meo et superior summo meo."[32]

---

[29] Dreher, 33.
[30] Dreher, 104.
[31] Dreher, 184.
[32] *Confessions*, III, 6, 11.

INDEX OF NAMES